W9-BYN-121

Carlo Ranzi

SEVENTY MILLION YEARS OF MAN

With illustrations by the author

Greenwich House
Distributed by Crown Publishers, Inc.
New York

Acknowledgments

The author wishes to thank for the kind assistance given him in placing at his disposal the fossil collection and the university libraries: Prof. E. Borzatti von Löwenstern, Institute of Anthropology, University of Florence; Dr. A. Manfredini and S. Cassano of the Museum of Origins, University of Rome; Dr. A. Mangili, of the staff of the Zoological Garden and the Museo civico di Zoologia del comune di Roma, Rome; Prof. P. Passarello, Institute of Anthropology, University of Rome; Dr. M. Zei of the Center for Studies of Quaternary Ecology, Florence; and Dr. C. Brain, Director of the Transvaal Museum, Pretoria, South Africa, for the help and encouragement given him throughout his task.

The author further wishes to thank all who have supported and followed his work with interest, above all Rita and Franck Vanderplank, Johannesburg, for the bibliographical research executed at the Transvaal Museum of Pretoria, South Africa.

To Claudio and Cecilia

Copyright © 1982 by Rizzoli Editore-Milano
English translation copyright © 1983 by Rizzoli Editore-Milano
All rights reserved.

This 1983 edition is published by Greenwich House,
a division of Arlington House, Inc.,
distributed by Crown Publishers, Inc.,
by arrangement with Rizzoli Editore.

Manufactured in Italy

Library of Congress Cataloging in Publication Data
Ranzi, Carlo, 1933–
   Seventy million years of man.
   Translation of: Homo settanta milioni d'anni fa.
   Bibliography: p.
   1. Man, Prehistoric. 2. Human evolution. I. Title.
GN740.R3613 1983   573.3   83-3916
ISBN:0-517-415984
h g f e d c b a

Preface

It might well be said that we are living in the age of photography. In the hands of young and old, men and women, the camera is used to document every moment of life and every important—or unimportant—event. There are countless snapshot albums that describe and record all the family happenings, both the interesting ones and the trivial ones, the happy ones and the sad ones.

However, no one so far has one very important album, an album which no camera has been able to produce: the album of the great human family from our remote common infancy up to the present.

From those distant days in which the fossil remains of our predecessors began to be recognized as such, we have been seeking, with varying fortune, to reconstruct our ancient appearance. Just think, there are some books published in the last century in which the authors, feverishly working over the discovery of a stone axe, succeeded in deducing not only the gait, size, and bodily characteristics of its creator but even his facial features! Clearly our grandfathers arrived at such results by following a logical, if debatable, train of thought; but it is equally obvious that fantasy and imagination have always occupied a prominent place in the field of prehistoric science.

A person going into a palaeontology laboratory nowadays would certainly be disappointed—rows of bone fragments set out on a big table, calipers, squares, goniometers, and sheets of paper covered with rows of numbers. The same scene would appear on another bench, this time covered with chipped stones and prehistoric artifacts. And in the center of the room, an electronic computer. Such laboratories have become the burial ground of fantasy; today every fact must be established mathematically and the various data must be accurately analyzed so that the results can be expounded with the utmost realism.

Is it possible for a student of human palaeontology, living in this kind of laboratory, speaking its language, and using its methodology, to reconstruct the irreparably lost human face or body (which consist of soft parts which cannot become fossilized), the muscles, hair, and skin of which we have never found any traces.

Cuvier was convinced that every part of an animal's body was so closely correlated with all its other parts that he could affirm categorically that a fragment of a limb was enough basis for a reconstruction of the appearance of the whole animal even if the species no longer existed.

The author of this work has obtained sufficiently reliable results by a meticulous anatomical study of the bony skeleton, of the muscles and their volumes, and by paying careful attention to the latest findings of modern primatology and comparative anatomy. The relatively few others who have followed independent paths have arrived at similar results, thus providing good confirmation of the author's work, which has, however, been carried further.

Hair and skin characteristics are realistic without exaggeration and well correlated with anatomical details and the climate and landscape in which the various types of Hominidae lived. The miming gestures and the psychological tension in the faces, the manifestation of a latent or definitely acquired humanity are the results of great experience and profound observation coupled with a marked sensitivity and lively facility of expression. The reconstructions of the surroundings and the particular events are very ably controlled, and the imagination never runs away from the facts as far as experts have been able to discover or deduce them from the fossil record. The author, regularly informed of the latest achievements of these disciplines, has merely enlivened the hypotheses in which scientists believe at present, describing their essential and most striking points.

A work like this might well appear risky to a scientist accustomed to the utmost accuracy in data processing and to the constant testing of theoretical deductions. This skepticism has been clearly justified in the past by the tendency to allow fantasy to fill up gaps or to take the place of facts where ideas were not yet clear. The author of this work has nevertheless managed to demonstrate that it is possible to express the truth with an artist's brush, used in such a well-balanced way as to add nothing and to leave nothing out.

I had this immediate sensation during an exhibition of prehistory organized in Rome in 1979. One day I noticed a very tall man hand in hand with a small boy gazing into a case containing some hominid skulls. I do not know how long they had been there examining various details of those ancient remains. Then, coming up to me, the man asked my opinion of some of his drawings which he carried in a portfolio under his arm. I saw then, between my hands, images literally torn from my deep subconscious; intangible and evanescent ghosts which I had many many times attempted to fix in my imagination assumed form and color at that moment on those sheets of drawing paper. "Excuse me," I said, "what is your name?" "Carlo Ranzi."

EDOARDO BORZATTI VON LÖWENSTERN

Drawing and Paleoanthropology

The activity of an artist, based on observation and intuition, and that of a scientist, based on research and description, are likely to complement each other. In the case of the natural sciences the artist's function is secondary. Because of their greater ability to depict prototypes and be informative, drawings are an improvement over photographs, but photographs can always be substituted. With paleoanthropology, on the other hand, drawing becomes an extremely useful complement, since the artist is called on to provide, by soundly based intuition, the kind of data which scientific treatment has not succeeded in extracting. Any paleoanthropological study contains a descriptive part, which is intended to allow one to visualize the external appearance, activities, and characteristic surroundings of the fossil relics or, more precisely, of the individuals to whom the relics belonged.

The abstractions of written language, which may provide meticulous indications of thicknesses, angles, dimensions, inclinations, and function do not, however, allow us to form a complete, accurate, and detailed enough picture of the particular object. Yet both the researcher and the layman feel the need to arrive in the end at a spatial image of the individual under observation, which will be an all-inclusive synthesis, immediately and completely perceivable, of the data as collected and confirmed.

This is the function of a specialist draftsman who, using all the data extracted by researchers in the field and after having in some way mulled them over by a kind of controlled and directed intuition, creates an all-around spatial synthesis of the data, thus satisfying one of the typical needs of those who use paleoanthropological research.

GENERAL CRITERIA

Anyone who sets out today to reconstruct the general external appearance of hominids or other archaic forms of the genus *Homo* can avail himself of three existing points of reference, each of which inevitably leads his work along certain lines.

The first of these is both concrete and tangible. It is furnished by the bony fossils which permit re-creation of the cranial structure in its various sizes, shapes, and characteristic postures. The exact identification of these elements and their correct interpretation allows the individual subject to be placed in a region which can be defined with some exactitude and which places itself in an intermediate position between the other two points of reference (equally tangible and concrete) formed, on the one hand, by the typical structure of contemporary man and, on the other, by the characteristics of contemporary apes. It is commonly accepted that these species represent evolutional terminals of descent from a single original species, and they are therefore parallel variants between which one can expect to find a very marked correlation. Thus one can reasonably suppose that more or less remote evolutionary stages of the human species will show considerable affinities with the present day forms of species of "ape." By placing the individual under observation in his rightful place between these two extremes and evaluating that position one can then decide whether his characteristics belong predominantly to the one or to the other of the two reference points.

The most reliable hypothesis will be that which, starting from the details of the finds, succeeds in integrating them in a correct mix of apelike and manlike attributes.

Reconstructions which are produced taking into account the points of reference mentioned above are obviously conjectural to a considerable extent, so much so that it is possible to work out many different variants, any one of which can be regarded as credible.

The three pictures on the facing page illustrate the complete succession of the artist's work: Starting from the fossil find, often damaged or incomplete (Fig. 1), he follows the fundamental guidelines which are described to him until he arrives at a justifiable version of the appearance of the whole bony structure (Fig. 2). This base must then be gradually and properly "clothed" with cartilage and a set of muscles (Fig. 3) and, finally, with its integument (skin and hair) to obtain a complete and convincing image whose appearance is situated at a suitable point between that of a contemporary man and an ape. Last, the artist must study the expressive possibilities, bearing in mind all the indications which local fieldwork has made available regarding the cultural attributes of the individual subject.

INTUITION AND IMMERSION

The artist who specializes in the paleoanthropological field is first of all an observer. He observes his fellows and learns how to reproduce and register all the dimensions, expressions, and gestures which characterize them and their culture. He also observes, whenever and by whatever means he can, the appearance, expressions, and gestures of the primates which constitute his other essential pole of reference.

Consciously or unconsciously he stores up facts and data and consciously or unconsciously compares and contrasts them mentally to identify that point of intersection between the two poles which corresponds to the subject of his choice, seeking always to define intuitively the external and internal pattern of the archaic human form which preserves traces of its animal ancestry while anticipating certain features of a more highly evolved humanity.

It is during this intuitive dialogue, fed with informative data and facilitated by a great familiarity with the fossils and other evidence but affected also by the prolonged and oscillating contemplation of the point of departure and the point of arrival, that the hybridization between the two extremes actually materializes. This is the ultimate objective of the oscillation; and the subject takes on its form based on known factual data supplied by science with dimensions originally schematic and approximate but then growing gradually more detailed and more precise until a dynamic and animated picture is created with its own specific way of living, perceiving, and expressing itself disclosed by its attitudes, facial expressions, and appropriately characteristic behavior.

The preliminary work described above serves to lay down the limits of justifiable assumptions. But this is not all. In the absence of much information, the quality and reliability of the final drawing also depends on the degree of psychological penetration it manages to reach. Part of the reconstruction is in fact born from the artist's ability to identify himself with the subjects and individuals he is picturing, "immersing" himself in their internal structures which in the case of beings with psychological attributes, are psychological structures, and representing them not as inert but as recognizably active. This procedure is absolutely indispensable when mimico-expressive attitudes have to be represented, since they do not depend only on the provision and placing of suitable muscles but also on the way this remote ancestor of ours perceived and faced up to the reality of his environment or, in other words, on his culture.

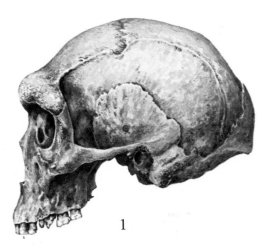

1

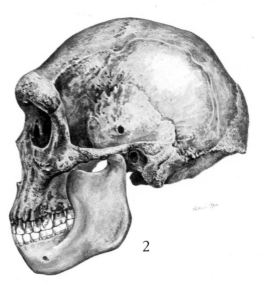

2

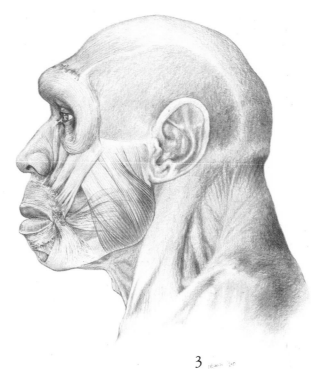

3

From "Studi per l'Ecologia del Quaternario" number 2/3–1980 Florence.

The Primates

According to the theory of continental drift, 200 million years ago all lands above sea level were gathered into one continent, called Pangaea. Later this mass broke up and subdivided into sections, which, sliding over the semifluid strata of the mantle below, became separate continental masses.

Here we see the probable appearance of the earth in the Mesozoic era, about 130 million years ago. Africa and South America are partially separated, while India, already split off from the southern block, has begun the movement which was eventually to join it to the coast of Asia.

The age of the dinosaurs came to an end 70 million years ago. In spite of the evolutionary success reached by reptiles in preceding epochs, many species were already extinct or were becoming so. A variety of events, among which the advent of mammals and a series of geological changes, irreversibly compromised the basic conditions necessary to their survival.

Mammals, which are warm-blooded animals, have an outer fur, which, by keeping a layer of air in contact with the skin, isolates their bodies from the atmosphere and so maintains a constant inner temperature.

The first mammals, favored by their smaller size and coats of fur, remained active even during the night, while cold-blooded reptiles lay in a state of torpor.

Derived from insect-eating mammals, the order of Primates became established toward the end of the Cretaceous period. The first known forms did not differ much from other mammals; however, in the course of their specific evolution, the primates were to give rise to some diversifications due to a predominantly arboreal way of life. The need to pursue their prey in the tree branches favored the increasing mobility of the forelimbs and the ability to grasp with hands and feet; to this must also be added a greater development of sight as compared to smell. The most ancient primate known today is the *Purgatorius Unio.* Only a few centimeters long, it owes its name to the locality in Montana where its remains were found. The layer goes back 70 million years.

8

The Evolution of Hominidae

The two most evident physical characteristics that distinguish man from the other primates are a constantly erect posture with habitual bipedal locomotion and increased cranial capacity with development in both volume and complexity of the brain.

Other important differences are the shortening of the profile of the face with respect to the cranium; smaller teeth; the perfecting of the hand which, from an organ of support and locomotion, became the principal instrument of human activity, able to manipulate and capable, to a certain extent, of expressing emotions and thoughts.

The existence of hominids in the Pliocene and Pleistocene is proved by some hundreds of fossil remains found in various parts of the world, but principally in Africa, Asia, and Europe. These remains make possible the reconstruction, in spite of some gaps, of the history of the evolution of man. This is the domain of paleoanthropology, a science which studies the beings that have lived on the surface of the earth in the course of geological time by means of those elements partially preserved as fossils in sedimentary rocks. Through this study, based on the age and on the recognizable characteristics of the remains, it aims at building up the geneological tree of the human species. The most important qualitative distinction between man and the primates is a cultural one, in the broad sense of the word: the ability to think and to speak, to acquire new knowledge, and to convey it to others.

There are no direct testimonies of this element in existence, and only by studying the prehistoric tools and implements which have come down to us can we hope to arrive, indirectly, at an understanding of the ability to reason and to communicate possessed by the hominids who made them.

This is why the data furnished by fossil remains have to be integrated with those obtained from the study of the tools and the environment in which they were produced, which is the field of prehistoric archaeology. The synthesis of the work carried out by the paleoanthropologist and the discoveries made by the archaeologist allows the formulation of some hypotheses on the behavior of hominids and on their evolution up to their present forms.

Not all the characteristics which distinguish hominids have appeared contemporaneously, nor have they evolved at an equal pace up to the present stage. This has been a long evolutionary process, whose final result—the appearance of man—has been reached gradually, without its being possible to isolate any significant stage or critical moment which has directly preceded the appearance of a definitely "human" being.

The accumulation of paleontological evidence indicates that different families of primates—Cercopithecidae, Pongidae, and Hominidae—all descend from one extinct and so far unknown progenitor. But only Hominidae have shown any tendency during the course of their evolution to acquire both an erect posture (with important consequences to the skeletal structure and the internal organs) and functional hands (to the extent of succeeding in making tools). Furthermore, added to these elements is a progressive increase in the size of the brain.

The remains of *Aegyptopithecus zeuxis* have been discovered in the El-Fayyūm region of Egypt. In spite of having a tail, it would appear (from the U-shaped dental arch and the presence of wide gaps between the canines and the incisors) to be related to the African Pongidae (presently represented by the gorilla and the chimpanzee).

In the *Propliopithecus haeckeli,* whose remains also come from the Oligocene layer of El-Fayyūm, it is possible to recognize certain characteristics—a less prominent face and a shorter dental arch than the Pongidae—which place it in the hominid evolutionary line, characteristics destined to stabilize during the evolution of man.

The Descent from the Trees

Many species of ape and monkey still spend the greater part of their lives in trees. Depending on their body structures, they move from branch to branch, using only their four paws or with the help of their tails. Sometimes they hang suspended from their hands and, by displacing them alternately, are able to move further. This latter method, known as brachiation, is practiced by gibbons, who carry out impressive acrobatics, and, in a less spectacular manner, by the chimpanzee. The gorilla, because of its great bulk, moves mostly on the ground, while the orangutan moves by displacing one limb at a time. Brachiation is often practiced at great heights and requires a capacity to judge, with a momentary glance, the distance between branches, their relative strength, and consequently, the possibility of grasping them with a strong, safe hold.

Food gathering territories which are generally arranged on horizontal levels allow different species of monkeys to move about in their search for food without interfering with each other, each species operating at a different level from the ground.

An arboreal life and a vegetarian diet are possible in tropical forests where seasonal changes are little noticed and food is plentiful throughout the year; whereas in the temperate zone, the greatly varying temperatures during the year cause the leaves to fall in the cold season with a consequent shortage of food.

It was precisely a climatic change which set off the next stage in the evolution of the primates. When the Indian continent (separated from Africa since the Triassic period) concluded its slow migration toward the North (during the Oligocene and Miocene, 35 to 25 million years ago), and its northern shore locked under the continent of Asia, causing the Alpino-Himalayan orogenesis, profound changes took place in the climate. In both Asia and East Africa it became colder and drier. The border of the rain forest receded toward the equator, leaving in its place a vegetation composed of sparse woodland, grassland, and savannah.

While the pongids remained confined to what remained of the forest, the hominids colonized the new environment, descending from an exclusively arboreal habitat to ground level in the glades and clearings and on open ground.

This event, which might have been a limitation, revealed itself instead as an extraordinary opportunity offered to those primates. In fact by exploiting on the ground the skills they had acquired in the trees, they succeeded in reaching an erect posture. By verticalizing the entire skeletal structure, brachiation had laid the foundations for the adoption of a semi-erect posture and bipedal gait. The ability to stand erect on the hind legs, even if limited to short periods of time, gave the hominids of the Miocene the opportunity to occupy new territory in which they were able to preserve the versatile movements of arm and hand and the capacity of grasping learned from moving among the branches, while the foot, with the gradual formation of the plantar arch, assumed the function of a pedestal, supporting the weight of the body.

Between the *Aegyptopithecus* and the living African pongids come the dryopithecids which were widespread in Africa, Europe, and Asia. Between 20 and 10 million years ago, these monkeys, progenitors of such modern anthropoids as the gorilla, the chimpanzee, and the orangutan, existed in a variety of forms and sizes. The African *Dryopithecus major (Proconsul)* was the largest of the dryopithecids species.

The ramapithecines were small primates which lived in Africa, Asia, and Europe in the late Miocene and in the Pliocene (14 to 10 million years ago). From their physical characteristics they could well be the progenitors of the australopithecines and of man.

A specimen of the genus *Ramapithecus punjabicus* came to light in the Miocenic outcrops of the Siwalik mountains, a pre-Himalayan chain on the northeast border of Punjab.

Ramapithecus reveals decidedly hominid characteristics, especially in the head. The face is moderately prognathous, the canine teeth are relatively small and the dental arch is without diastemata, the gaps between canines and incisors typical of the pongids.

The strength of the jaw and the molars speaks for a predominantly vegetarian diet based on seeds and tough herbs. Such indications of his environment as were found with him suggest he occupied a territory of swamp forest and grassland.

Ramapithecus had only occasionally to enter open land in search of food and always returned to the shelter of the woods.

The *Oreopithecus bambolii* found in the Upper Moicene lignite deposits of Mount Bamboli in Tuscany appears from the structure of the pelvis to have been capable, although still imperfectly, of bipedal locomotion together with its considerable capacity for brachiation.

The slightly prognathous face of *Oreopithecus* and its tendency to walk on two legs suggest an orientation toward hominid lines, but this group did not evolve further.

The denomination of *Gigantopithecus blacki* (on right) is well suited to this primate which lived in eastern Asia between the Upper Pliocene and the beginning of the Pleistocene (between 10 and 12 million years ago).

Because of its great bulk, which must have been at least twice that of the present-day gorilla, it must necessarily have lived on the ground; however the species was still confined to a forested environment.

The Miocene and Pliocene landscape was populated by primitive mammals whose forms, while belonging in their general characteristics to species living today, appear strange and unusual to us. The *Calicotherium* was a gigantic herbivore with a vaguely equine profile and paws provided with formidable claws; the *Sivatherium*, which resembled a member of the giraffe family with a short neck, had horns; the *Machairodus*, on the other hand, because of its characteristics, is also called the "saber-toothed tiger."

Kenyapithecus wickeri is considered to be the African form of *Ramapithecus*. Its remains, dated at 14 million years, are associated with lava pebbles which show signs of use and with antelope bones which appear to have been broken by a blunt object (perhaps the bones were broken to extract the marrow). This is the oldest evidence we have of the use of an instrument on the part of a hominid.

The *Australopithecus afarensis,* known by the nickname of Lucy, was discovered in 1974 at Hadar in the Afar territory in Ethiopia (now the Republic of Djibouti).

This was a find of exceptional completeness, of a specimen of *Australopithecus,* a genus which includes a large group of hominids living in Ethiopia and the Transvaal from 7 to 2 million years ago. Fossils found on the surface practically always consist of isolated fragments: jaws, teeth, skulls, those parts, in fact, strong enough to withstand the action of predatory animals at first and then atmospheric agents. But of Lucy there have been found about two-thirds of the entire skeleton (with parts still anatomically connected) of a female about 20 years old.

Lucy proves irrefutably what has been widely surmised in the past regarding other fossils, numerous but fragmentary, from Tanzania and from South Africa: the acquisition by *Australopithecus* of a definitely erect posture.

The finds discovered near the territory of the Afars and those of Laetoli represent strong evidence of the physical appearance of the most ancient forms of *Australopithecus*.

In the Laetoli Plain, 25 miles south of Olduvai, a couple of australopithecines left a track in the ash deposited by an eruption of the Sandiman volcano. In the conformation of the footprint, dated about 3 million years old, it is possible to recognize a human-type foot with the toes aligned and a plantar arch suitable for supporting the weight of the body.

Two million years ago in the vast Serengeti Plain (Tanzania), at a much lower level than nowadays, there was a lake on the banks of which a band of australopithecines was encamped. In relatively recent times, in this region which has been subjected on a number of occasions to violent volcanic phenomena, a wide fissure has opened in the ground: the Olduvai Gorge. Sedimentation from the ancient lake, buried by an eruption of the volcano Olmoti, is visible in the walls.

The savannah is a stretch of level grassland, dotted with shrubs and groups of
trees such as acacia, euphorbia, and baobab.
It was on land such as this that the hominids of the Miocene and the early Pleistocene, having once acquired erect stance,
established themselves with the object of
procuring food by hunting.

Australopithecus

In 1924, Professor Raymond Dart extracted the fossilized skull of a primate of the apparent age of 6 to 7 years from a limestone breach at Taung, South Africa. In spite of the difficulties inherent in determining a species on the basis of a single specimen, and especially that of an infant, Dart unhesitatingly baptized his fossil with the name *Australopithecus africanus* (South African Monkey), claiming it to be of a different species from the other known primates.

Later, between 1936 and 1938, in the Sterkfontein mine, also in South Africa, Robert Broom found numerous remains of adult specimens which not only confirmed Dart's hypotheses, but also helped to define the appearance of the Australopithecines.

The shape of the pelvis and the relationship between the head and the spinal column make it possible to establish that these primates had definitely acquired an erect posture and that their bipedal locomotion was perfected with respect to their Miocene predecessors. They are of smaller size although relatively robust: 44–66 pounds (20–30 kilograms) of weight for a height of 3½–4 feet (110–120 centimeters).

The profile is still apelike, with receding chin and forehead; but the volume of the brain case, which reaches 500 cubic centimeters, is greater than that of the largest present-day apes. The teeth indicate a strong tendency toward omnivorous feeding. Having become habitual visitors to the savannah, the australopithecines of the early Pleistocene integrated their vegetarian diet with the meat of the small animals they hunted.

We ask ourselves what resources, if not behavioral ones, would have made it possible for *Australopithecus* to compete against the impressive natural weapons of the animals of the savannah.

The use of fragments chipped intentionally from animal bones, both as tools and as weapons, has been attributed to the australopithecines of Makapansgat in the Transvaal (*Australopithecus prometheus*). This has apparently been confirmed by the presence of a number of baboon skulls broken by blows in the same layer of sediment. Not all scholars agree in recognizing the culture, which from the materials used (bone, teeth, and horn) has been called osteodontokeratic.

In order to survive, *Australopithecus,* having neither tusks nor claws, made up for their absence by using stones and clubs.

Having become a hunter, *Australopithecus* is assumed to have lived a social life ruled by complex relationships coordinated by a system of communication made up of signs and sounds.

The ecological chain of the savannah: a large feline kills an antelope . . .

. . . the remains of the antelope, abandoned by the main predator, are consumed by carrion eaters (hyenas and vultures).

Australopithecus, attracted by the large prey but incapable of killing it, takes the antelope from the jackals, his feared competitors, and succeeds in chasing them away.

The exploration of the sedimentary deposits of Africa along the River Omo and near Lake Turkana (ex-Lake Rudolph) and those in Tanzania and the Transvaal give evidence of the existence of two forms of Australopithecines: *Australopithecus africanus,* considered "gracile" and *Australopithecus robustus (Paranthropus robustus).* This latter fed mainly on substantial, fibrous vegetable matter.

The robust *Australopithecus* is distinguished from its "gracile" counterpart by its larger stature (5 feet/1½ meters) and greater muscular strength. If its appearance generally resembles the hominid model (the structure of the hand and erect stance), the shaping of the head presents several pongid characteristics, such as a jaw which is particularly massive and heavy due to energetic mastication and the absence of a forehead.

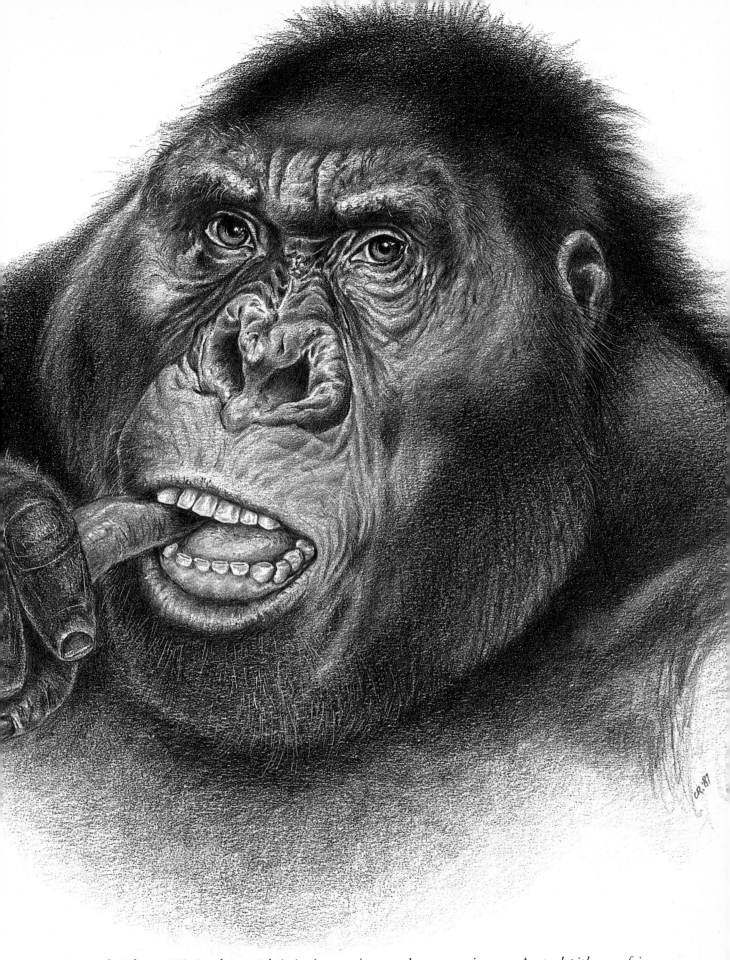

Australopithecus (Zinjanthropus) boisei: the subspecies *boisei* represents the final adaptive stage of *Australopithecus Robustus*, which it surpasses in height and ponderous size. Living at the same time as *Australopithecus africanus* and *Homo habilis,* it did not evolve, and 1 million years ago it became extinct and left no trace.

37

The English anthropologist Louis S.B. Leakey was born in Kabete, Kenya, in 1903 and died in London in 1972. He is noted above all for the numerous discoveries he made in collaboration with his wife, Mary, in the Olduvai Gorge. Leakey made a fundamental contribution to the story of evolution; furthermore, we owe to him the discovery of the remains of *Proconsul* (1948), *Zinjanthropus* (1959), and *Kenyapithecus*.

Although he has not been the only one to make important contributions to paleoanthropological science, his dedication to the work and his capacity for instilling his own enthusiasm in all who met him created an almost legendary halo around him and his family which is associated with pioneering days and now with field research.

Homo Habilis

The first man appeared on the African scene two-and-a-half million years ago. Hominids with erect stance, the australopithecines of the savannah, had prepared the way.

The genus *Homo* was assigned to the specimen discovered by Louis Leakey in Stratum 1 of the Olduvai Gorge in 1960. The bones found there were associated with the remains of animals killed and eaten on the spot and with a number of roughly shaped lava utensils. It was the evidence of intentional toolmaking that determined the genus *Homo* and the species *habilis.*

Discoveries made in the following years, also in the Olduvai Gorge and at Koobi-Fora on Lake Turkana, contributed to the complete definition of all the characteristics of the first man. Compared with *Australopithecus,* from which his physique is inherited, *habilis* is distinguished for his greater weight and stature; the morphology of his pelvis and of his foot appears to be more advanced, and he seems to walk and run with equal facility; his cranial capacity is much higher: 530 to 750 cubic centimeters.

His most distinctly human element, however, is seen in areas which are decidedly cultural, indications of which are supplied by various archaeological discoveries: a stone technology, documented in numerous localities, and the beginnings of a social structure, which can be read from the hut bottoms or the floors of dwelling places (*living floors*) of the Olduvai Gorge and Melka-Konturè in Ethiopia.

The most important consequence of an erect stance is the liberation of the hands from the need to assist in locomotion. Even more than the brain, it was the hands which reaped greater and more immediate benefit from the new condition.

In the structure of the upper limb of a primate, one can observe how the bony sections, beginning with the shoulder, multiply in number and decrease in size until, in the case of the finger, they become a series of finely articulated segments. The australopithecines exploited the potential capacity of such a structure, accomplishing the essential functions of prehension and of tactile investigation. In brachiation, the monkey's hand carries the weight of its body hanging from the branches. Long and slender, the hand is used as a hook, leaving a merely contributory function to the short, curved thumb. The differently proportioned hand of *Australopithecus* has a longer thumb which bends inward toward the palm and can take a tight hold with the coordinated action of all the fingers.

The *Homo habilis* (K.N.M. 1470) of Lake Turkana

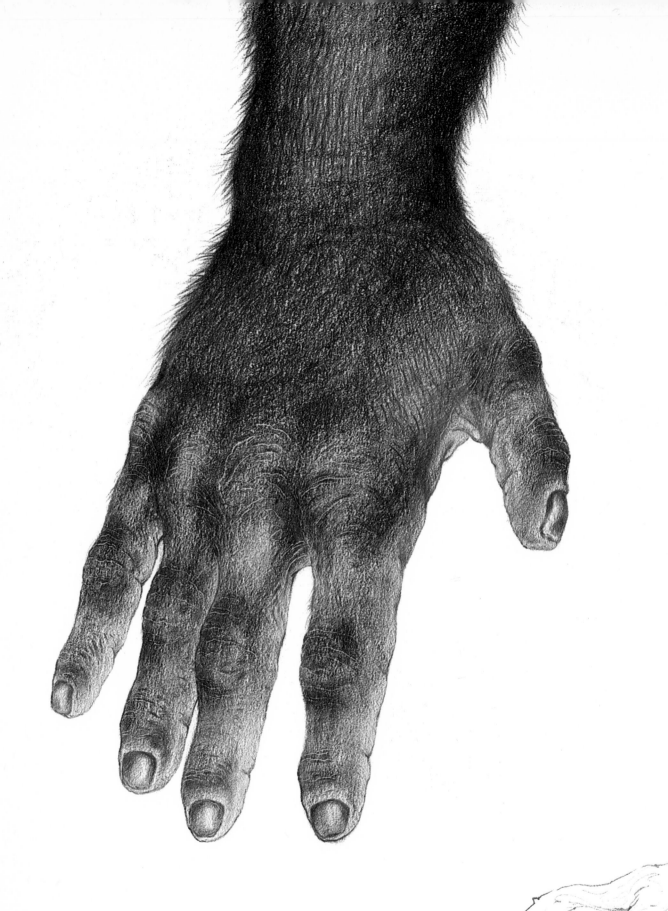

The advent of a firm grip, added to an elevated capacity for tactile discrimination, marked a decisive turning point in hominid evolution and opened the way to more complex forms of manipulation.

When a pebble is held in two hands and struck with great force, pieces flake off. Sharp cutting edges are formed between the broken and the original surfaces. Thus, in the most simple form, the first instrument conceived and made by man, was born. A series of tools made in this way without any further refinement came from Stratum 1 of the Olduvai Gorge; they are dated at 1 million 850 thousand years. Pebble industry, or Olduvaan culture, also used a flaking technique which consisted of striking blows with a stone held in one hand, and was called hard percussion, or hard hammering.

Among the animals hunted by *Homo habilis* were mammals of the genus Deinotherium, now extinct pachyderms, which had downward-curved tusks. *Homo habilis* lived in a hut built of dry twigs or a perimeter of stones.

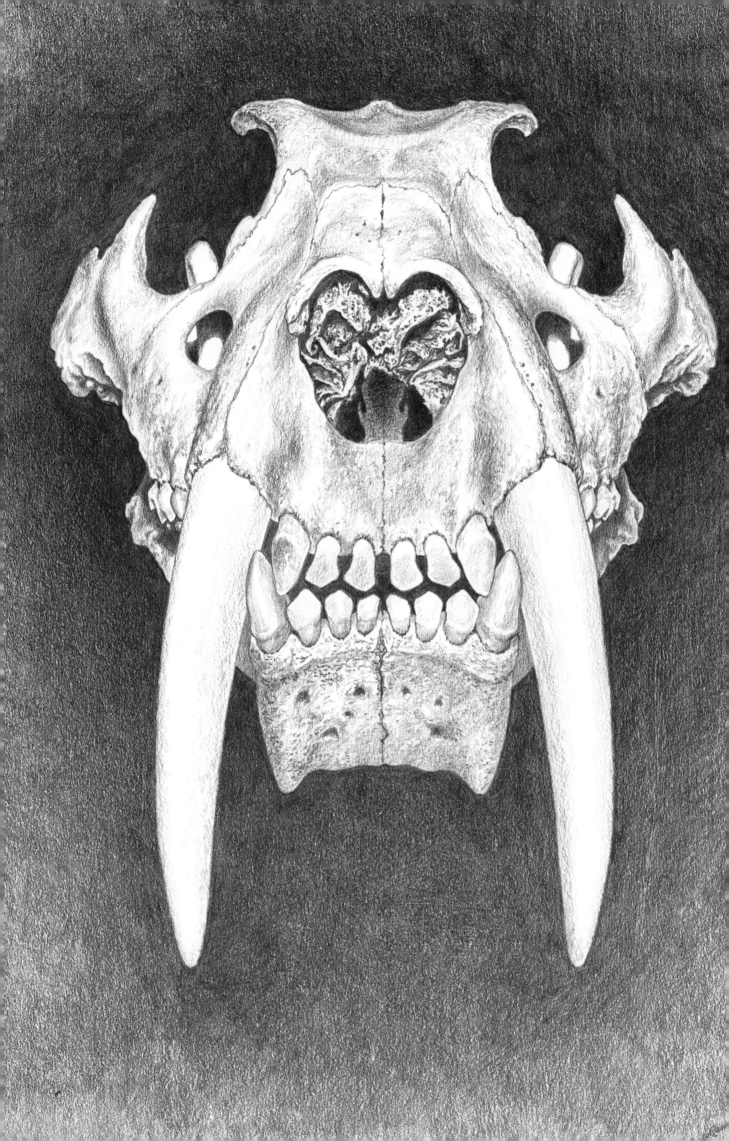

The Saber-Toothed Tiger

Primitive man had numerous enemies. From his first appearance on the face of the earth, when he already looked substantially different from the other primates, he was forced, from time to time, to defend himself from the rigors of the climate, from the scarcity of food, and from other more powerful and better-armed animals. Among these, there emerge the terrifying images of the carnivores with saberlike teeth.

Widely diffused in the Old and the New World, and subdivided into various species of different sizes but similar habits, these animals were already present in the Miocene when little *Ramapithecus* appeared. And while the human species evolved, rich and dynamic in its changing forms for millions of years, the large felines, relatively stable in appearance, vied with them for the role of predator.

The remains of one of these felines, belonging to an animal of the *Machairodus* genus, have been found in the sedimentary deposits at Vertesszöllös, Hungary; it is dated at about 350 thousand years. Both strong and extremely able the *Machairodus* had the highly developed senses typical of its family. Nevertheless its salient characteristic was its teeth, impressive, highly developed upper canines, which, in the largest specimens, reached lengths exceeding 8 inches (20 centimeters).

Its method of attack seems to have been similar to that of snakes: the jaw, which could drop low enough to assume a vertical position, allowed the animal to open its mouth to enormous size and free the huge sharp canine teeth, which it used like daggers to spear the prey with a sudden downward jerk of the head and neck. In this way the animal killed its prey, of which it then probably consumed the internal organs, leaving the carcass to the hyenas and jackals.

Although encounters between man and the largest saber-toothed tigers were probably only occasional, since their respective fields of action only partly overlapped, the medium-size specimens must have included him among their possible prey.

A spontaneous question arises here: what resources had man to fall back on; what defensive strategies, rocks or clubs, or group actions could he use to compete with so physically well-endowed an adversary? The results of such contests must most often have been fatal.

Homo Erectus

Over 2 million years ago there appeared on the earth a hominid form which combined all the evolutionary tendencies manifested up to that time and already outlined in *Homo habilis: Homo erectus.*

If the australopithecines had acquired bipedal locomotion and in *Homo habilis* the functionality of the hand had been developed, in *Homo erectus* it was the volume of the brain which showed the greatest advance, reaching values of between 800 and 1000 cubic centimeters. The face still retained certain pongid characteristics while the body resembled that of present-day man.

Stone industry is characterized by a rich and multiform instrumentation; next to the pebbles which recall pebble culture, one finds the ax with a transverse blade, knives and scrapers made from flakes chipped off in working, and bifaced hand-axes. In the oldest hatchets the cutting edge, obtained by knocking on the two faces with a heavy stone instrument, is wavy and irregular. In the next phase, the bifaced knives were much more refined thanks to the adoption of an important technical innovation: the soft hammer. This is a blunt instrument made of wood or bone, which, used to chip off smaller pieces, made it possible to obtain a straighter edge. A 20-foot-thick (6 meter) layer of ash and carbonized animal bone found in the caves of Choukoutien indicates a controlled use of fire. *Homo erectus* had at last learned to put to his own advantage one of the elements which, until that time, had been among the most hostile of his habitat. Once he had overcome the animalesque panic, fire became for him an invaluable auxiliary instrument.

It would appear that the organization and coordination of complex social activities such as hunting, documented in the deposits of Torralba, Spain and Olorgesailie, Kenya, can have been possible only with some form of communication. The coordinated action of a group of hunters bent on making a successful attack on a herd of large and dangerous animals, such as elephants or baboons, calls for the ability not only to conceive but also to lay down a plan of action, to assign individual responsibilities and indicate the successive phases of the operation. One can imagine, therefore, that *Homo erectus* had developed some form of communication which depended not only on gesture but also on the formation of simple articulated sounds.

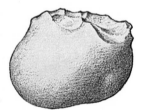

Vallonet (France)

Olduvai (Tanzania) Stratum 2

Olduvai (Tanzania) Stratum 2

Choukoutien (China)

Olduvai (Tanzania) Stratum 2

North Africa.

The *Pithecanthropus* of Modjokerto, Java.

The *Pithecantropus* of Lantian, East China.

The *Pithecanthropus* of Trinil, Java.

Sinanthropus observes the fire.
It was probably seeing branches accidentally burning that gave *Sinanthropus* the idea of making use of fire.

In tropical zones the mildness of the climate and the abundance of vegetable resources provided *Pithecanthropus* with relatively favorable living conditions.

The points of javelins are hardened in the fire.

Skillful blows shape the stone axes.

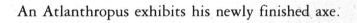

An Atlanthropus exhibits his newly finished axe.

Although *Sinanthropus* was not capable of lighting fires, he had learned how to preserve the embers. Ash deposits in the caves of Choukoutien demonstrate how he made use of fire to give heat, to protect himself from wild animals, and to cook food.

Two specimens of *Sinanthropus* dragging home the kill. Collaboration between the hunters became essential elements for the successful conclusion of a hunt.

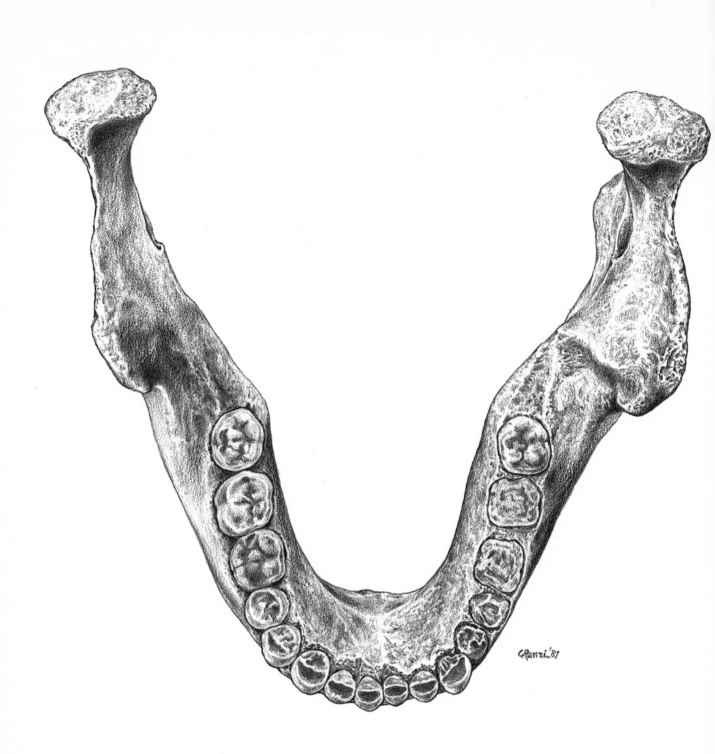

The Mauer jaw, found in an alluvial deposit in the old bed of the River Neckar at Mauer, near Heidelberg in Germany, goes back to about 700 thousand years ago and is therefore the oldest human fossil found in Europe up to this time. The size of the jaw, which is of a heavy archaic shape, somewhat exceeds the average among remains of *Homo erectus,* while the shape of the dental arch and the morphology of the individual teeth are very advanced and similar to those of modern man. The structure and robustness of the jaw, almost abnormal in some respects, lead one to suppose that it belonged to an individual of exceptionally massive proportions who lived in a warm-temperate climate.

A Mauer man pauses to look at the skull of a rhinoceros.

A nocturnal encounter at Olorgesailie.

The Man of Terra Amata

The remains of a paleolithic camp of 300 to 400 thousand years ago came to light in 1966 in a locality known today by the name of Terra Amata, on the outskirts of Nice. The settlement was situated on a fossil beach, 100 feet (30 meters) above the present level of the Mediterranean, and the complex consists of the bases of oval-shaped huts from 25 to 50 feet (8 to 15 meters) long. The perimeter of the dwellings was marked by stones of medium and large dimensions, while traces of holes for supporting piles can be detected in the floor. We suppose that the walls were constructed with interwoven branches.

Toward the end of the Mindel glaciation the climate in this region was less rigid and hostile than in other parts of Europe, and a crown of mountainous spurs sheltered the bay of Terra Amata from the more severe winds blowing from the Northeast. A nearby spring ensured a supply of fresh water, while molluscs, turtles, and small fish were fished both from the sea and from the bed of the river (now the Paillon) which flowed near the encampment.

The fauna of the zone must have been rich and varied. It can be inferred from the remains of food abandoned inside the huts that the hunters attacked young specimens of large mammals, such as elephants and rhinoceroses without however neglecting smaller prey.

The stone-tool industry of Terra Amata, which used beach pebbles rolled smooth and rounded, included hand axes (crudely flaked at one end only), axes, points, awls, and scrapers. Some bone tools were also found, as were a few "pastels" of red ochre and a round print left, perhaps, by a bowl-shaped container.

The prehistoric site of Terra Amata has not given up any human bone remains. If the dating and the archaeological context attribute the site to a species of *Homo erectus,* nothing remains of these ancient hunt-

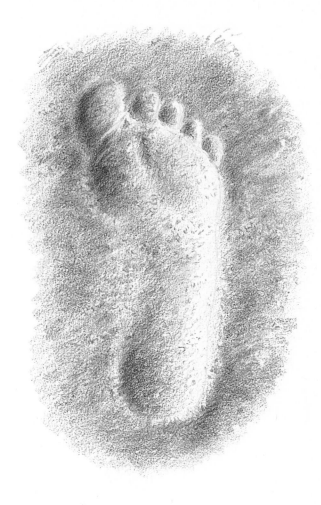

ers but the imprint of a right foot impressed on the sand. The trace, 9½ inches (24 centimeters) long, represents the only testimony to the physical appearance of the men of Terra Amata.

The great mass of archaeological evidence produces a vivid picture of the daily life of its inhabitants. The superimpositions of inhabited layers demonstrates that the hunters stayed several times on this beach, sheltered from the wind, on the trail followed when hunting game. Because of its vegetation and great wealth of raw material suitable for toolmaking, this position certainly represented an ideal place for a large group not only of hunters but also of women and children to reside.

Terra Amata. Two men arriving in sight of their dwellings on their return from hunting.

The interior of a dwelling in Terra Amata;
while the women tend the children, a man
renews the supply of tools.

On the edge of the River Paillon.

Presapiens

During the interglacial, between the Mindel and Riss glaciations, a human population with more developed characteristics than *Homo erectus* spread through Europe; one example is the Steinheim man whose remains were found in the locality of that name in Germany.

During the Mindel-Riss interglacial, the animal population in the environs of the River Thames included, among others, rhinoceros, deer, and boar. These animals were hunted by Swanscombe man.

The remains of a *Presapiens* belonging to a contemporary and similar species (in terms of general characteristics) to that of the German skull found at Steinheim, have come to light at Swanscombe in the south of England (Kent). Some aspects of the morphology of the head, common to both, indicate characteristics found in the later *sapiens*.

The stone-tool industry of the Swanscombe site consists principally of symmetrical bifaces well finished with a soft hammer.

67

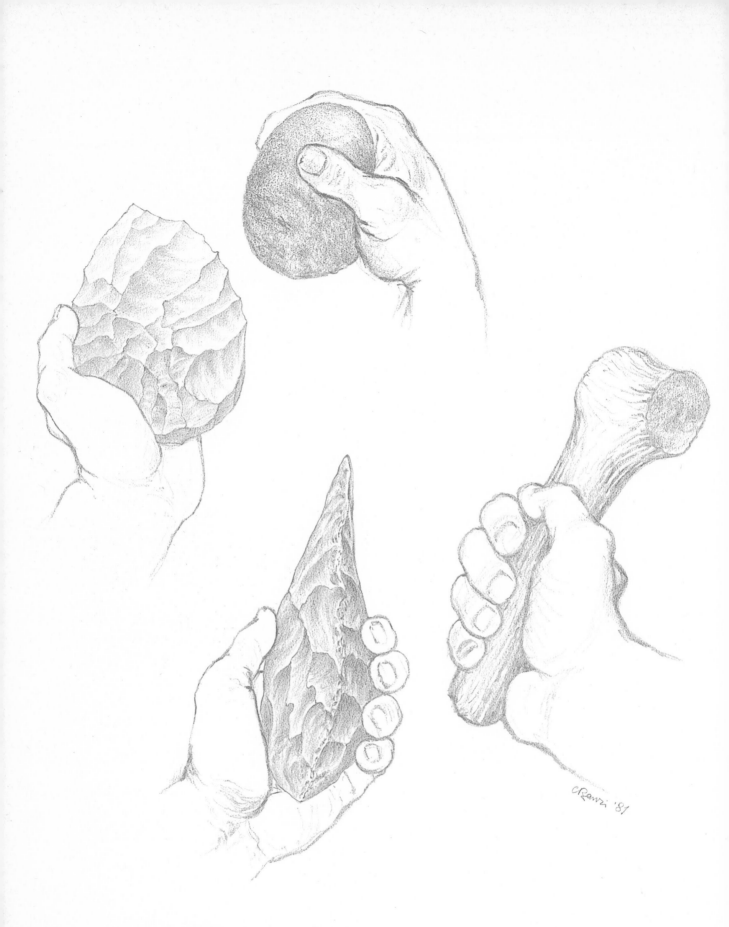

A specimen of the Acheulian industry: the kidney-shaped flint is roughly shaped with a hard stone alternately on the two sides; the cutting edge is then made even and perfected by knocking with a soft hammer of horn or of very hard wood.

68

The third, or Riss, glaciation was the most widespread and the longest; Antarctic type glaciers invaded the Northern hemisphere and pushed their long tongues down to the lowest latitudes ever recorded.

In spite of the frigidity of the European climate, the periglacial zones were occupied by men who managed to survive by hunting the mountain animals that descended to the lower terrain.

During the third glaciation the caves in the Pyrenees were occupied by a highly evolved Archanthropus, a hunter of ibex: Tautavel man (Arago man).

The cave of Lazaret, situated in the back country of the south coast of France, was inhabited during the Riss glaciation. To shelter themselves from the intense cold, the occupants erected a type of bulkhead, probably composed of planks of wood supported on piles of stones, which still remain.

The floor shows traces of fires and sleeping pallets; a wolf's skull was found on a rock near the entrance.

The Arctic wolf was hunted by the men
of Lazaret, who used the fur for blankets.

During the Riss-Würm interglacial period the climate improved. On the Italian peninsula, where temperatures were higher than those of the present time, some localities such as the valley of the River Aniene at the gates of Rome contained extensive swamps.

Among the Riss-Würm populations, of particular interest were those living in the tropical belt, such as Solo man (Java). Certain archaic characteristics persisted in his physiognomy. Perhaps at some stage in his evolution, the environment in which he lived was so favorable that no physical adaptation was needed.

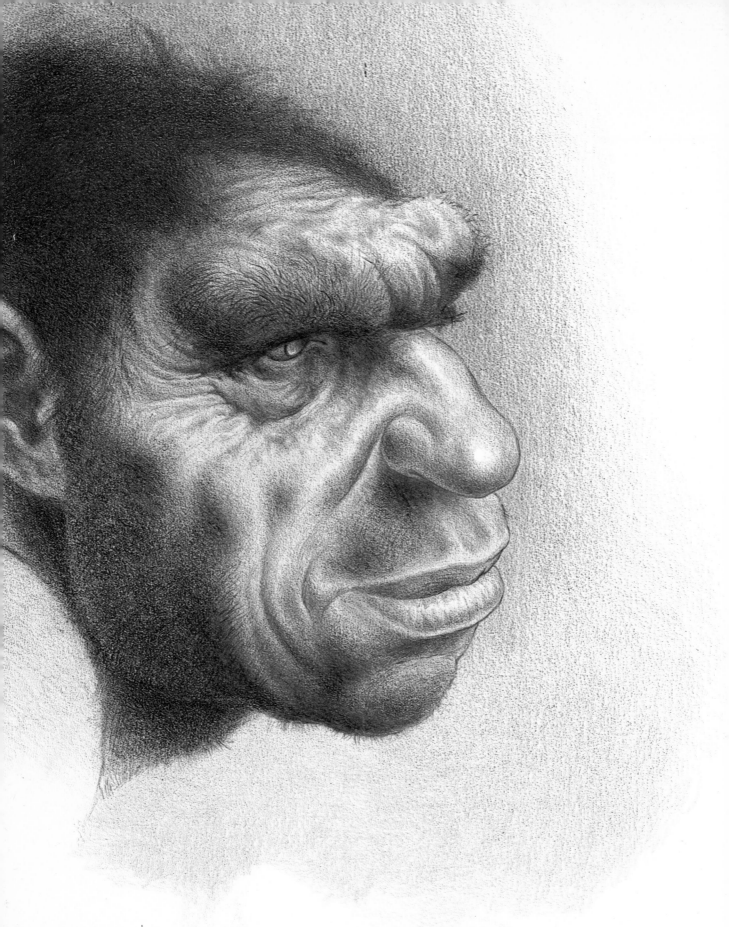

Broken Hill man was found in eastern Rhodesia. A study of the remains indicates that the head had a number of strongly archaic characteristics which recall the *Pithecanthropi*. However, the large volume of the brain—1208 cubic centimeters—and the modernity of the postcranial skeleton recall the particular characteristics of the *Paleanthropi*, which spread throughout Europe in the course of the fourth glaciation.

Saldanha man, of the South African Riss-
Würm interglacial had a massive build. As
a hunting weapon he used granite spheres
which he probably swung around in the
manner of the Argentine gauchos.

77

Neanderthal Man and the Fourth Glaciation

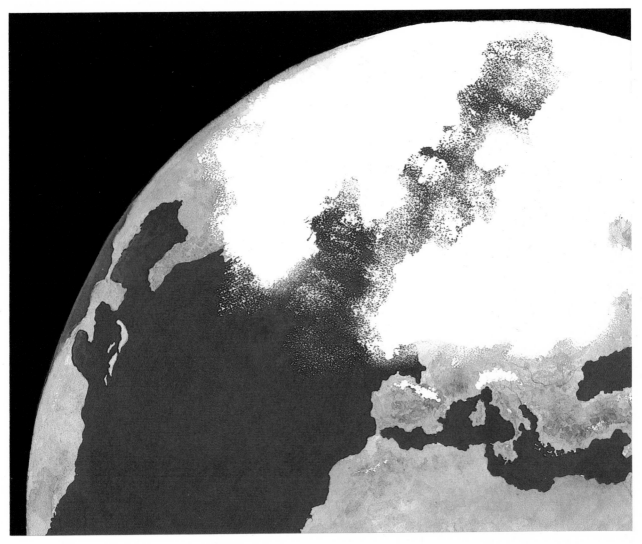

About 75,000 years ago a further climatic alteration gave place to the fourth, or Würm, glaciation. Enormous quantities of water were subtracted from the oceans whose average levels dropped by 260 to 330 feet (80 to 100 meters). The seas underwent important phenomena of regression and some of the sea beds emerged, greatly modifying the coastal outline to that with which we are now familiar. Neanderthal man lived during the first half of the fourth glaciation. He belonged to a race of massive, thickset individuals, considered to be one of the points of maximum physical adaptation reached by the human genus.

Neanderthal skulls have huge brow ridges above the eye sockets, receding foreheads and chins, and strong jaws; the cerebral volume is very high (1681 cubic centimeters for La Ferrassie 1), and the profile of the occipital bone shows a characteristic prominence. In some respects Neanderthal man appears to have reached a high degree of culture. This is proved not only by the large-scale adoption of a complex and sophisticated procedure for flaking stone (known as the Levallois technique), but above all by the practice of burying their dead. The numerous burials with prearranged positions for the deceased, accompanied by offerings of objects and food and the episodes of ritual cannibalism attribute to the Neanderthals the ability to express a high level of thought. The conception of some form of existence projecting beyond death also goes back to them.

Neanderthal man was not only a cave dweller; encampments in the open and shelters under overhanging rocks have also been documented.

The Neanderthals were more widely diffused than could possibly be deduced from the bone remains alone; the levels of occupation which have produced evidence of the typically Neanderthal stone-tool industry known as Mousterian cover a very extensive area.

The persistence of the highly specialized
characteristics of the western Neanderthals
over time was probably due to genetic isolation, which was forced upon the people by
the difficulty or impossibility of migratory
movement via the narrow belt which had
been created by the drawing together of the
Scandinavian and Alpine glaciers.

Although present in older archaeological sites the technique known as Levallois was adopted and used to a large extent by the Neanderthals.

A series of small triangular points, the famous Levallois points, were obtained from the nucleus after it had been roughly shaped and prepared.

Hunted, probably with the help of a trap, the great woolly rhinoceros was one of the most sought-after preys of Neanderthal hunters.

Some Neanderthal populations were exposed to polar temperatures. Although there is no documented evidence of sewing techniques, it is generally supposed that they used the furs of animals to make cloaks and footwear.

Men and bears fought for possession of the caves to shelter them from the rigors of the climate. The gigantic cave bear *Ursus Spelaeus* could be attacked at the end of its hibernation when, still weak and sluggish, it was unable to defend itself.

Purposefully deposited bear skulls have led to the belief that a bear cult was practiced by Neanderthal man.

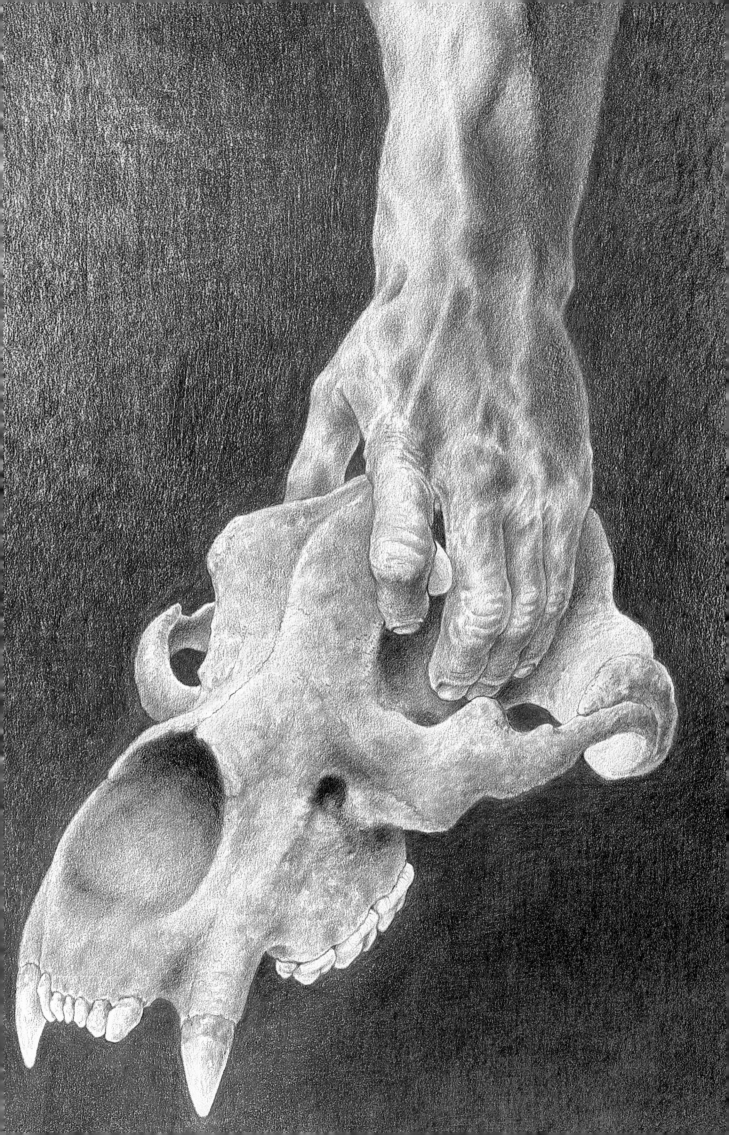

The prolonged need for maternal care and
the children's dependence on adults must
have favored the growth of very strong ties
of affection between mother and child.

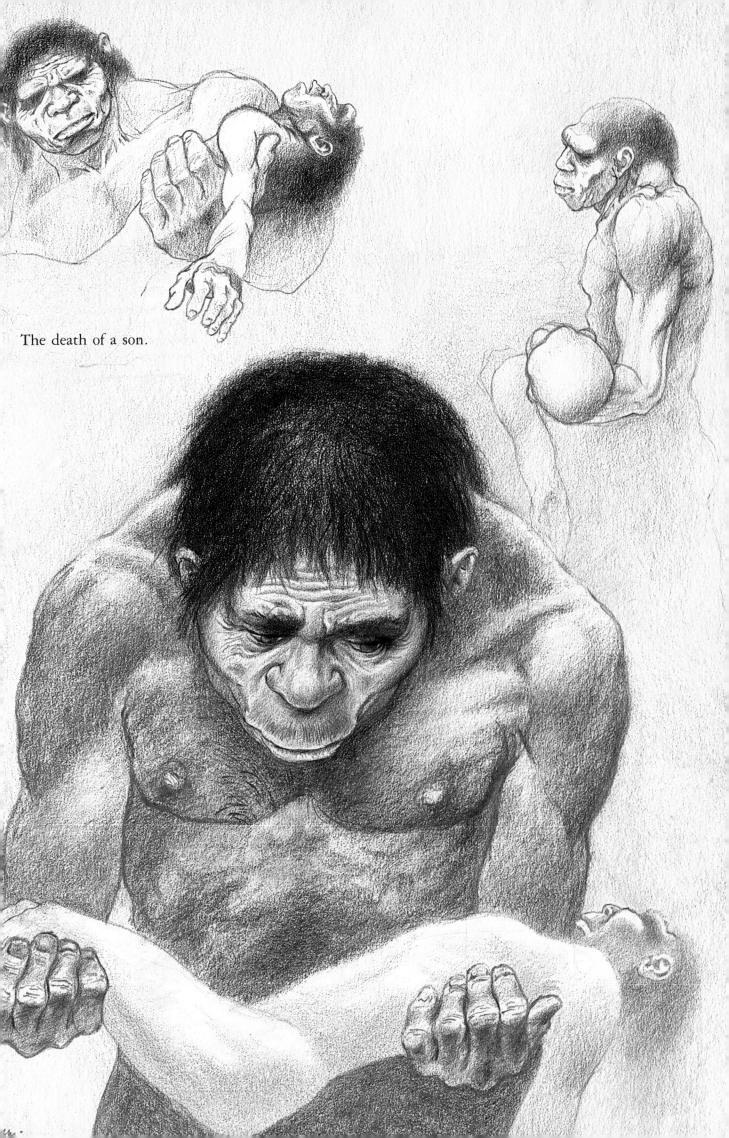

The death of a son.

We know that the man of Monte Circeo,
a Neanderthal of the Tyrrhenian coast of
Italy, was killed by a blow on the right
temple.

After death, at the end of a complex magical-propitiatory ritual, his skull was placed in the center of a circle of stones in an obscure recess in the Guattari Grotto, which was named after its discoverer.

In 1957 a Neanderthal burial, dated at about 45,000 years, was discovered in the Shanidar cave, in eastern Iraq. The analysis of fossilized pollens found in the sediment showed that the deceased had been laid on a bed of wild flowers. A second important discovery brought to light an aspect of the social behavior of the Neanderthals: at the time of his death the man of Shanidar had lost the use of one eye and of his right arm. His condition proves that, in spite of his being disabled, the man had been cared for and kept alive by the solidarity of his companions.

Ochre and mallow for the dead companion.

About 40,000 years ago the caves in the sides of Mount Carmel in Palestine were inhabited by a group of humans whose characteristics were transitional between the European Neanderthals and the more advanced Cro-Magnons.

The typical Neanderthals disappeared from the European scene about 40,000 years ago. Numerous hypotheses, all equally credible, have been advanced to explain this disappearance: isolation, epidemic, extermination.

The first evidence to come down to us of the formulation of abstract thought—the techniques of working flint, burial, a few marks of obscure significance carved on pebbles—are owed to Neanderthal man.

All this is the expression of a culture which was truly his and which survived him, being passed down to the men of Cro-Magnon.

93

Cro-Magnon Man

Starting about 35,000 years ago, the Neanderthals were gradually replaced by a human species with very different physical traits—the people known as Cro-Magnon.

Because the Cro-Magnon is practically indistinguishable from living humans, it is classified as *Homo sapiens fossilis,* while contemporary man is classifed as *Homo sapiens sapiens.* Both subspecies are grouped under the name *Neanthropi,* new men.

The denomination Cro-Magnon was used generically to define races and varieties very different in physical type and origins. They are, in fact, conspicuous in the finds at Combe-Capelle and Mentone, France, Oberkassel, Germany, and Předmostí, Czechoslovakia.

The individuals of French type were generally robust and tall and can be distinguished from the Neanderthals by important modifications in the conformation of the head. The transformation of the cranium is accompanied by an increase in the frontal lobes of the brain, where important functions connected with conceptual relationships are controlled. Furthermore, archaeological finds associated with *Neanthropus,* such as weapons, utensils, ornaments, and artistic representations present proof of a capacity for abstract thought, which, already demonstrated in the Neanderthal culture, reached even higher levels.

Toward the end of the fourth glaciation, the culture of the last hunter-gatherers became extinct and the way was opened, about 10,000 years ago, for other forms of adaptation. Favored by the temperate climate of the large land areas left exposed by the glaciers, the advent of agriculture and established settlements laid the foundations for the urbanization and the first historical civilizations of man.

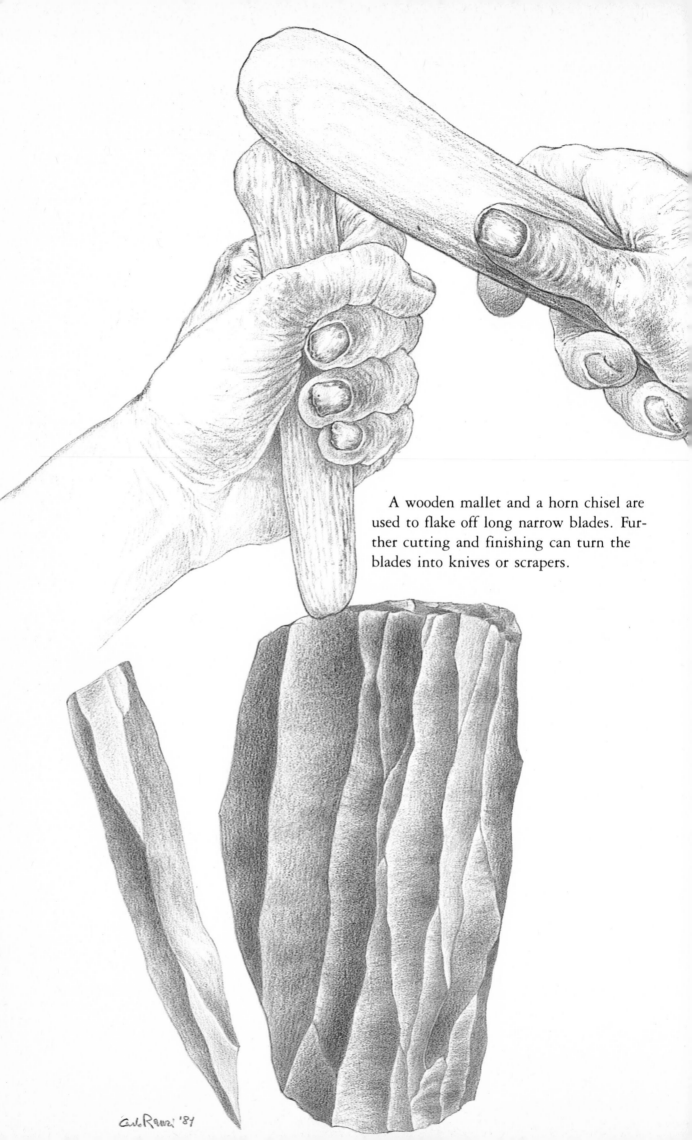

A wooden mallet and a horn chisel are used to flake off long narrow blades. Further cutting and finishing can turn the blades into knives or scrapers.

The reindeer is an animal adapted to the life in low-temperature environments. During the Würm glaciation large herds of reindeer populated the tundra which cov-ered a large part of Europe in regions which have a temperate climate today. Highly prized prey of paleolithic hunters, they were often represented in paintings and graffiti.

The hunters of mammoths on the Siberian tundra obtained not only food and furs from their prey but also material for building their huts. Their need to protect themselves from the temperature, which in winter could fall to 60 degrees below zero Fahrenheit (50 degrees Celsius) as well as the scarcity of trees and the difficulty of chopping them induced the northern plain dwellers to develop an unusual method of construction with which they built dwellings large enough and comfortable enough to shelter an entire family group.

A circle of skulls, interrupted only at the entrance to the dwelling, with the tusks still fixed in their sockets, constituted the perimeter and the external ribs of the hut, while other bones stuck in the ground served as reinforcement for the load-bearing poles. The walls consisted of a series of blade bones overlapped to form an almost continuous surface; skins and leafy branches must have completed the covering of the walls, which were reinforced at the top by a mass of reindeer antlers. Various hearths were provided both inside and outside the huts. Archaeological excavations of the floors have brought to light numerous objects indicating the culture of the mammoth hunters. Among the finds of bone and ivory are pierced needles and awls, probably used for making clothes, and small statuettes of females; ornaments such as bracelets, necklaces, and pendants were also found.

In spite of the prohibitive cold and the difficulties of hunting the great herds of pachyderms, everyday life in such a community must have been lived in a certain degree of comfort and allowed for the pursuit of some activities not strictly connected with survival. We have proof of this in finely executed sculptures and graffiti on ivory, an artistic expression in which the themes of hunting and fertility frequently recur.

The woolly mammoth was a common elephant in Europe and Asia during the fourth glaciation. Ten feet (3 meters) tall, it had large curved tusks and was covered by a thick fur of reddish hair 1 foot (30 centimeters) long with a mane 2 feet (50 centimeters) long.

A group of huts with fireplaces, dated 28,000 years ago, has been found at Dolni Věstonice in Czechoslovakia. A great number of mammoth bones, the remains of meals, and flaked flints had been abandoned in a refuse deposit on the outskirts of the village.

A short distance from the habitations an isolated hut with a large central kiln was found. It contained a number of statuettes modeled in clay and powdered ivory; the images represent animals and female figures, one of which is very well-preserved. While the stylization adopted by the sculptor only roughly indicates the face and limbs, it emphasizes the breasts and stomach, elements which lead one to think of a pregnancy and fertility cult.

The Venus of Dolni Věstonice.

The remains of no fewer than 10,000 horses have been found under the cliffs of Solutré in France. To kill them, paleolithic hunters drove the herds up to and over the edge of the cliff.

The Solutréan culture, which goes back 14,000 years, produced stone instruments of extremely high quality; the flint blades were sharpened by means of a series of parallel flakings: thus the blades named "willow leaf" and "laurel leaf" were born.

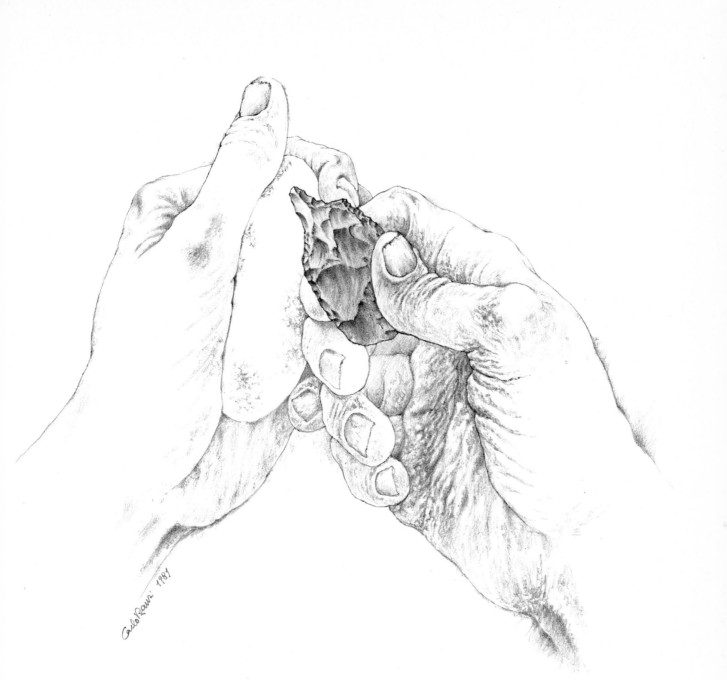

The shaping of the utensils was often finished by rubbing the edge with a finishing tool of stone or bone; the chipping off in this way of minute flakes no longer than fish scales can be compared with a true and proper sharpening. Using the pressure finishing tool and generally starting with a leaf-type blade, the Solutréan hunters succeeded in making awls and drills of exceptional fineness.

A deer of great size lived during the Upper Pleistocene. Distinguished by large antlers, which could attain a width of 10 feet (3 meters), it was highly prized as prey by the paleolithic hunters.

In the Grotto of Naux, an unknown master-artist who lived about 10,000 years ago has left us one of the finest examples of paleolithic art.

The invention of the bow and arrow goes back about 10,000 years. At the same time that man, exploiting the energy inherent in wood bent with great force, was relieved of the need for a direct encounter with his prey, there appeared at his side the first examples of the domesticated dog.

A paleolithic knife: a flint
blade inserted into a
bone handle.

107

Around 5,000 B.C. man profoundly modified his way of life and his economy, transforming himself from a hunter-gatherer into a farmer and breeder. During this period stone working reached the height of perfection with the final smoothing and polishing.

Battle axes of various shapes, decorated with engravings, reveal in their execution a high aesthetic value, which is not always equalled by their functionality.

The Bronze Age and the Alphabet

The fifth millennium before our era, marked the slow gradual dying of the Stone Age. It was followed by what is generally called the Bronze Age, when bronze was used for tools and weapons. By 1500 it had spread to all Europe, India, and China. Superb examples of daggers entirely fused in bronze come from the Central European cultures.

The people of Phoenicia, navigators and merchants, were forced by their own commercial needs to simplify and stylize the existing methods of writing, establishing a conventional symbol for every articulated sound.

Thus it is to the Phoenicians that we owe the first alphabet. A flexible and easily understood system, it was largely used for writing commercial and administrative documents.

In the ninth century B.C., a Phoenician merchant had a temple raised in honor of the god Pumaï, near the present-day city of Nora, in Sardinia.

The name Sardinia (Sardana) appears for the
first time in the stele at Nora, the oldest
Phoenician inscription found in the Western Mediterranean area.

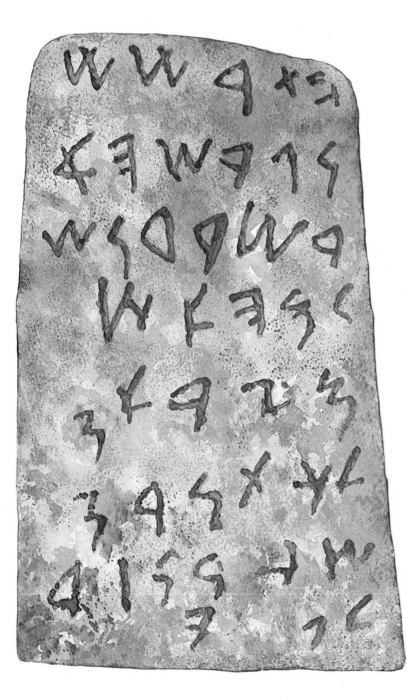

1. TEMPLE OF THE CAPE OF

2. NUGAR WHICH IS

3. IN SARDINIA. LET IT BE

4. PRESERVED

5. COMPLETE. (THE) STELE WHICH

6. MELEKYATON HAS BUILT

7. WHICH (THE TEMPLE) THE PRINCE
HAS BUILT

8. IN HONOR OF PUMAÏ.

The Stones Are Millions of Years Old

This book has come to an end. The products of art and technology and the invention of the alphabet, which are all prodigies achieved by man's intellect, tell us that cultural factors have definitely prevailed over activities connected with survival. The time when man, armed with stones and sticks, was heavily committed to the conflict with a hostile environment has passed and with it the basic ambience of prehistory.

In relation to the millions of years which have slipped away since an ancient primate, an obscure progenitor of man, decided to abandon the trees where it had been living to venture on to the ground, the millennia of written history constitute the last bit of a long spiral, a small portion whose lineaments, furthermore, are well known. The chapters of that history pertaining to human evolution are sparse and fragmentary; and to attempt to compile, in an organic manner, a history of man which goes back to the appearance of the first trace of humanity, one must depend on the remains of bones and archaeological finds.

In every epoch the mystery of our origins has occupied our curiosity; at times, when visiting a museum of anthropology, someone will have seen his own image reflected in the glass of a showcase and will have tried to superimpose it, nose to nose, on one of the skulls on exhibition. The astonished look, the hesitant smile, sometimes an echo of a secret drama emerges from the shadow of the shelves. Letting oneself meet with their eloquence, the one vital and ringing, the other static and remote, but no less compatible for the traces of humanity present in both, one will have obeyed the impulse to recall those remains to life or, better still, the individuals to whom the remains belonged, taking them out of their resentful silence and even more from that sense of death which hangs fatally around in the museum collections of anthropological sciences.

Human evolution has probably not yet ended, but since men of the Cro-Magnon imposed their dominion over the earth, nothing in man has changed except, perhaps, thought: although he has shown himself capable of great speculation, the many questions remaining unanswered have left him profoundly perturbed.

If it seems to you that in the writing of this book the millions of years (quantities which in truth are beyond our ability to comprehend) have been too lightly bandied about, think again, because our planet is truly ancient: those stones which we, in the manner of the lords of creation, thoughtlessly trample, are broken fragments of the primordial scene in which the miracle of life began and, later, humanity emerged—those stones are millions of years old.

Appendices

Glossary

ABBEVILLIAN INDUSTRY Stone-tool industry of the Lower Paleolithic period, named after the gravel quarry at Abbeville in France. This period is characterized by the production of flaked instruments and coarsely worked hand-axes with uneven edges; the base was often left with the natural surface of the pebble. The accompanying fauna (*Elephas meridionalis; Machairodus*) places Abbevillian culture at the beginning of the Quaternary.

ABSOLUTE CHRONOLOGY Determination of the number of years which separate a terrain or fossil from the present time.

ACHEULIAN INDUSTRY Stone-tool industry of the Lower Paleolithic, named after the deposits of Saint Acheul in France. The typical instrument is the hand-axe, entirely flaked on both faces (bifacial) with a stone hammer and then finished with a soft hammer of bone or horn. The duration of the Acheulian culture was considerable: from the Mindel glaciation of the Riss-Würm interglacial. At Ternifine (Algeria) in 1954, C. Arambourg found a jaw bone of *Homo erectus* associated with an Acheulian biface instrument and axes.

AMYGDALINE See *Bifacial*.

ARCHANTHROPUS Fossil hominid recognized by E. Dubois in 1891 at Trinil on the island of Java. *Archanthropus* represents a higher evolved type of *Australanthropus* and includes the species of *Homo erectus* generically called *Pithecanthropus, Sinanthropus,* or *Atlanthropus.* Widely diffused all over the Old World, the most ancient of Archanthropines go back to the Lower Pleistocene; they are believed to have discovered and introduced the systematic use of fire for domestic purposes.

AUSTRALOPITHECUS Fossil hominid recognized by R. Dart in 1926 in the locality of Taung in South Africa. Denominated *Australopithecus africanus,* it is well known today thanks to the numerous discoveries in the Rift Valley deposits in Africa. Subdivided into two forms, one gracile and one robust, the australopithecine family had an erect posture. The gracile species was omnivorous.

One variety of *A. robustus* is classified *A. boisei.*

A developed australopithecine known to have been capable of making tools is classified as *Homo habilis.*

AWL A bone instrument with a pointed end, suitable for drilling holes.

BIFACIAL An instrument, most often almond-shaped (amygdaline), but also oval or triangular, made by flaking a stone nucleus on the two opposite sides until a cutting edge is obtained. Bifaced flaking was known throughout the Middle and Lower Paleolithic periods.

BLADE Stone implement, its length at least twice its width, flaked off by means of indirect knocking on the edge of the nucleus.

BRACHIATION Locomotion in suspension, using the arms only, typical of anthropoid monkeys and particularly of gibbons.

BROW RIDGE Bony protuberance of the cranium, which constitutes the upper edges of the orbits. Highly developed in apes and in fossil hominids but practically absent in present-day man.

CHOUKOUTIEN Village situated to the southwest of Peking, China. The limestone deposit, about 165 feet (50 meters) thick was excavated from 1921 to 1939 by J. G. Andersson, D. Black, O. Zdansky, W. C. Pei, F. Weidenreich, Teilhard de Chardin, and others. From this layer numerous remains were brought to light of a type of Archanthropus—25 adults and 15 youths—classified at first as *Sinanthropus pekinensis* and later grouped under the name *Homo erectus.* The deposit includes numerous sites of which the most important are: the site or "Locus 13" of the Mindel glaciation from which comes a flaked pebble; Site 1, of damp-temperate climate, of the Mindel-Riss interglacial from which come the bone remains; Site 15, of a cold dry climate of the Riss glaciation from which comes a more developed industry with large flakes and bifaced tools. The use of fire is indicated by a layer of ash about 20 feet (6 meters) deep. There are proofs of a stone-tool industry, using flaked pebbles of quartz and sandstone. The accompanying fauna includes the feline *Machairodus,* elephants, rhinoceros, and deer.

CLACTONIAN INDUSTRY Early tool industry from Clacton-on-Sea, Essex, England. Includes rather large flakes with prominent conchoidial fractures caused by violent blows. A rare find, a wooden javelin point, is also of the Clactonian period. It overlapped the end of the Abbevillian culture.

COMBE-CAPELLE (man of) *Neanthropus* found in 1909 by O. Hauser, in a grotto in the Dordogne region of France; considered to be a variety of the Cro-Magnon man from which it is distinguished by its

smaller stature and by the heavy archaic outline of its cranium. It was lying in a grave, wearing ornaments made of sea shells. It is dated between 30 and 35 thousand years ago.

CONCHOIDAL FRACTURE A fracture characteristic of flint: the curving and the development of the bulbar surface are related to the force of the blow and to the type of instrument used.

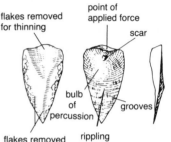

Schematic drawing of a Levallois flint

CORTEX Raw, often scored, external surface of a block of stone. Work was often begun on a flint nodule by removing the cortex. In the case of the Abbevillian ax, prehension of the implement is improved by retaining the cortex.

CRANIUM Skeleton of the head; contains the brain; organs of sight, hearing, and smell; and a mobile bone, the jaw. The shape, dimensions, and proportions relative to the various parts of the cranium are important to the determination of the evolutionary phase of the species. One can deduce from how far back on the cranium the first cervical vertebra (atlas) is connected the more or less erect posture of the skeleton.

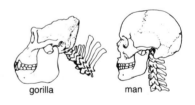

gorilla   man

CRO-MAGNON MAN *Neanthropus* found by L. Lartet in 1868 in a grotto on the outskirts of the village of Les Eyzies-de-Tayac, Dordogne, France, in the valley of the River Vézère. The find consists of 5 buried skeletons characterized by their height and the modern morphology of the cranium.

DENTAL ARCH Shape of the set of teeth. In apes the premolars and molars are arranged in two more or less parallel lines; the diastemata eventually to be filled by the voluminous canine teeth can clearly be seen. In man and in fossil hominids, the dental arch has a parabolic form, with rather diverging branches; there are no diastemata, except in the phase of replacement of the milk teeth around seven years old, due to the relatively small size of the first teeth compared with the development of the jaw.

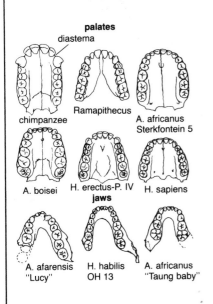

palates
diastema
chimpanzee
Ramapithecus
A. africanus Sterkfontein 5
A. boisei
H. erectus-P. IV
H. sapiens
jaws
A. afarensis "Lucy"
H. habilis OH 13
A. africanus "Taung baby"

DIASTEMA Space between the canines and the incisors and between the canines and the premolar teeth in the jaws. Always present in monkeys, diastemata do not occur in man or in fossil hominids whose teeth fit closely together.

FLAKING The operation of removing small pieces from a block of stone; it was practiced by prehistoric man for the construction of implements and utensils. The flaking was done by various methods of hammering and knocking to scale pieces off a pebble and shape it into usable instruments—hand-axes—or by shaping the nucleus to form a suitable knocking surface with which to form a series of points and blades of predetermined shapes—Levallois points. The waste pieces, with or without further working, were often themselves used as tools.

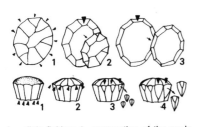

Levallois flaking: 1. preparation of the nucleus; 2. thinning; 3. Levallois flake.
1–2 preparation of the nucleus; 3. thinning; 4. Levallois points.

FLINT Silica rock which breaks with a conchoidial fracture, often found in the form of nodules, distributed in horizontal beds or strata. It was the raw material preferred by prehistoric man for the construction of artifacts.

FOSSIL Trace, imprint, or remains of a vegetable or animal organism which lived in past epochs. Chemical processes of substitution can mineralize the organic substances and preserve their form.

FRANKFURT HORIZONTAL Plane of orientation of the cranium; represented in the lateral sense by a line joining the lower edge of the orbits to the auditory canal.

GEOLOGICAL ERAS Subdivisions of geological time. The Precambrian era from which the formation of the earth dates (5 thousand million years), was followed by the Paleozoic, the Mesozoic, the Cenozoic, and the Neozoic or Quaternary which is still in progress.

GLACIATION Period characterized by the cooling of the terrestrial globe and expansion of the glaciers. The phenomenon has been repeated several times in the history of the earth; at least two glaciations are known to have occurred in the Precambrian and three in the Paleozoic eras. Four glaciations occurred in the Quaternary. They are known by the names Günz, Mindel, Riss, and Würm. The intermediate phases (interglacials) with warm or temperate climates are called Günz-Mindel, Mindel-Riss, and Riss-Würm. During the greatest extension of the Quaternary glaciers, a large part of Europe and North America was covered by an ice cap.

HAMMER A hard stone implement for working flint; its use can be recognized from the marks left by the beating. There are records of hammers for direct hammering and of others to be interposed between the stone to be worked and the direct hammer. Conchoidial fractures of small dimensions lead one to imagine the use of horn, bone, and wood.

HOMINIDS (hominidae) Family of the order Primates. Includes the genuses *Ramapithecus*, *Australopithecus*, and *Homo* (*habilis*, *erectus*, and *sapiens*).

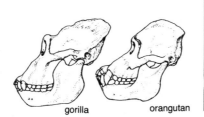

gorilla   orangutan

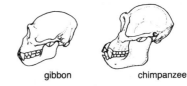

gibbon   chimpanzee

HOMINOIDS (hominoidea) Superfamily of the order Primates. Includes the families Hylobatidae, Pongidae, and Hominidae.

HOMO ERECTUS See *Archanthropus*.

HOMO HABILIS See *Australopithecus*.

HOMO SAPIENS NEANDERTHALENSIS See *Paleanthropus*.

HOMO SAPIENS See *Neanthropus*.

KIDNEY Flint pebble.

K.N.M.-E.R. Sign of possession and of provenance of the fossil remains at the museum of Nairobi. Kenya National Museum, East Rudolph.

LA QUINA Middle Paleolithic deposit situated in the Charente region in France. Excavated by G. Chauvet from 1872 to 1882 and by Dr. H. Martin from 1905 to 1936, it produced a Mousterian stone-tool industry and, in 1911, two examples—a female adult and a child—of Neanderthal man.

-LITHIC Of stone or pertaining to stone.

LOTHAGAM A locality near Lake Turkana (ex Lake Rudolph), in Ethiopia. A presumably hominid jaw fragment dated between 5 and 6 million years ago was found there.

LUKEINO A locality in Kenya near Lake Baringo, where a molar tooth of an *Australopithecus* dated at 6½ million years was found.

MAMMALS Class of the type of Chordates. Characterized by a body covered with hair, a system which permits control of the internal temperature (homeothermia), and mammary glands for feeding their young which are born alive but not autonomous.

MESOLITHIC Period of transition in the working of stone, which falls between the Paleolithic and the Neolithic. It corresponds to the phase of passage from a hunting and gathering economy to a production economy based on agriculture and cattle breeding. Mesolithic industry found favorable climatic and environmental conditions in the Middle East for its foundation some 10,000 years ago.

115

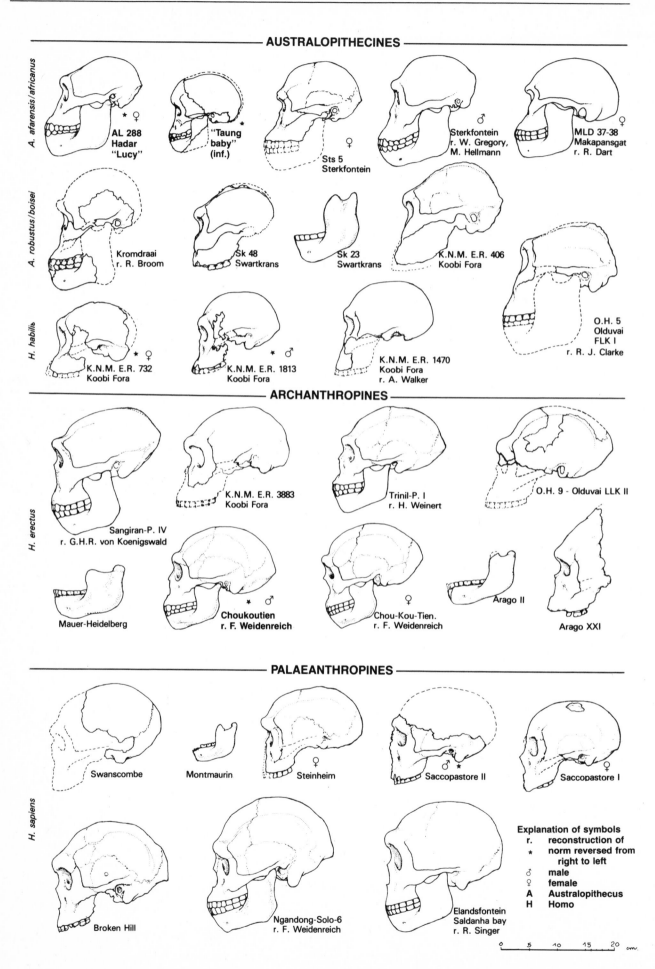

AUSTRALOPITHECINES

A. afarensis / africanus

AL 288
Hadar
"Lucy" ♀

"Taung
baby"
(inf.)

Sts 5
Sterkfontein ♀

Sterkfontein
r. W. Gregory,
M. Hellmann ♂

MLD 37-38
Makapansgat
r. R. Dart ♀

A. robustus / boisei

Kromdraai
r. R. Broom

Sk 48
Swartkrans

Sk 23
Swartkrans

K.N.M. E.R. 406
Koobi Fora

O.H. 5
Olduvai
FLK I
r. R. J. Clarke

H. habilis

K.N.M. E.R. 732
Koobi Fora ♀

K.N.M. E.R. 1813
Koobi Fora ♂

K.N.M. E.R. 1470
Koobi Fora
r. A. Walker

ARCHANTHROPINES

H. erectus

Sangiran-P. IV
r. G.H.R. von Koenigswald

K.N.M. E.R. 3883
Koobi Fora

Trinil-P. I
r. H. Weinert

O.H. 9 - Olduvai LLK II

Mauer-Heidelberg

Choukoutien
r. F. Weidenreich ♂

Chou-Kou-Tien.
r. F. Weidenreich ♀

Arago II

Arago XXI

PALAEANTHROPINES

H. sapiens

Swanscombe

Montmaurin

Steinheim ♀

Saccopastore II ♂

Saccopastore I ♀

Broken Hill

Ngandong-Solo-6
r. F. Weidenreich

Elandsfontein
Saldanha bay
r. R. Singer

Explanation of symbols
r. reconstruction of
* norm reversed from
    right to left
♂ male
♀ female
A Australopithecus
H Homo

0   5   10   15   20 cm.

116

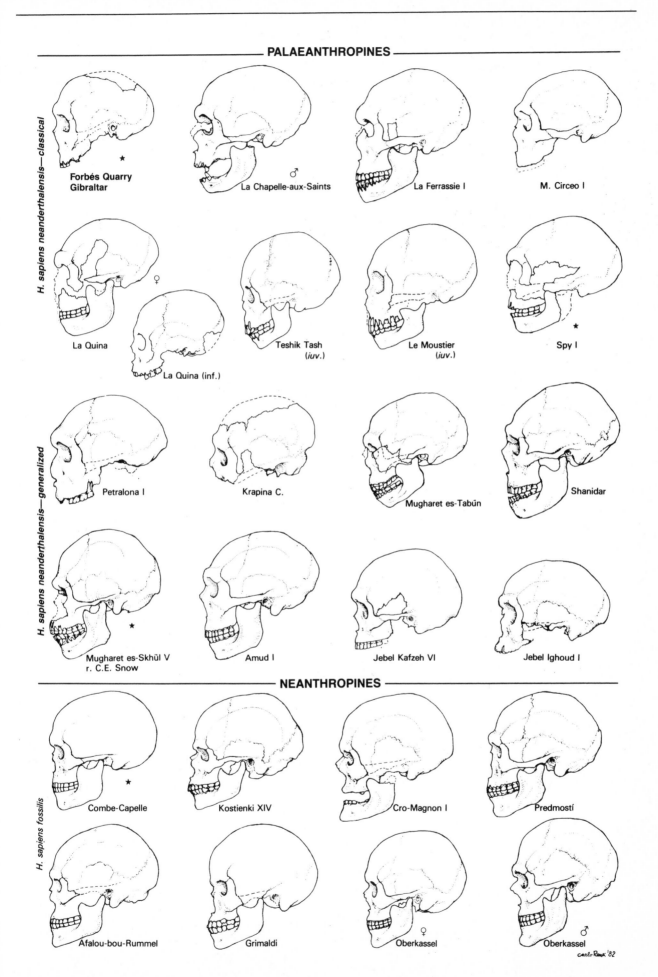

PALAEANTHROPINES

H. sapiens neanderthalensis—classical

Forbés Quarry
Gibraltar ★

La Chapelle-aux-Saints ♂

La Ferrassie I

M. Circeo I

La Quina ♀

La Quina (inf.)

Teshik Tash
(*iuv.*)

Le Moustier
(*iuv.*)

Spy I ★

H. sapiens neanderthalensis—generalized

Petralona I

Krapina C.

Mugharet es-Tabûn

Shanidar

Mugharet es-Skhūl V
r. C.E. Snow ★

Amud I

Jebel Kafzeh VI

Jebel Ighoud I

NEANTHROPINES

H. sapiens fossilis

Combe-Capelle ★

Kostienki XIV

Cro-Magnon I

Predmostí

Afalou-bou-Rummel

Grimaldi

Oberkassel ♀

Oberkassel ♂

carlo Rossi '82

117

METALLURGY From the fourth millennium B.C. metal working advanced alongside the Neolithic stone industry. Pure copper was used, followed by bronze, a copper and tin alloy. Casting metals in stone molds came to be considered the most economic method of producing series of durable and efficient objects.

MOUSTERIAN INDUSTRY Stone-tool industry of the Middle Paleolithic era. It takes its name from the rock shelter of Le Moustier, France. In the prehistoric station, excavated by E. Lartet in 1864, the skeleton of a Neanderthal was found and also a typical collection of instruments based on triangular points and scrapers. On the basis of such association, the archaeological sites with artifacts from the Mousterian culture are attributed to Neanderthal man.

NEANTHROPINAE Form of the genus *Homo* which appeared in Europe with the race of Combe-Capelle, France, 35,000 years ago. Practically indistinguishable from the races living at present, the neanthropines include both the fossil forms which lived in the second half of the fourth glaciation, and the present forms, diffused throughout the world ever since 10,000 years B.C. With the Neanthropinae there took place the passage from subsistence depending entirely on hunting to more complex forms of social organization, culminating in the advent, between the seventh and the sixth millennium B.C. of the first agricultural civilizations. The realization of a series of rock paintings (Lascaux, 15,000 years ago) of great artistic value is owed to the neanthropines.

NEOLITHIC The final period of stone working, noteworthy for the finishing and polishing of the tools. The first Neolithic cultures, based on the cultivation of fields and cattle breeding, appeared in the Middle East in the seventh millennium B.C. and, via the Valley of the Danube, spread throughout Europe. The sedentary way of life, due to an agricultural economy, brought about the formation of permanently inhabited centers, equipped with silos and kilns. The invention of ceramics and weaving were important innovations.

OMO Fossiliferous river region in the South of Ethiopia. The oldest worked pebble, dated at between 2 and 2½ million years, was found here in 1969.

PALAEANTHROPUS Fossil hominid of a more advanced evolutionary stage than *Archanthropus*, diffused throughout the Old World. The most ancient forms, or *presapiens* go back to the Mindel-Riss in-terglacial period. The Neanderthaloid palaeanthropines, so-named after the specimen found by C. Fuhlrott in 1956, in the Neander Valley in Germany, can be divided into two populations: the "specialized" or "classic" one established in France and in Italy in the first half of the Würm glaciation; and the "generalized" one of the Middle East. The first intentional burials and the Mousterian stone industry are both attributed to the Neanderthals.

PALEOLITHIC A term, created by J. Lubbock in 1865, which defines the flaked stone age, an archaeological period which goes back to the beginning of the Quaternary era. The chronology of the Paleolithic era has been studied successively by E. Lartet in 1863, by G. de Mortillet in 1872, and by Abbot H. Breuil in 1932. On the basis of recent studies, the Paleolithic is divided into three periods: Lower, Middle, and Upper.

The Lower Paleolithic began with the first flaked pebbles, which go back at least 2 million years and are attributed to African australopithecines. In the Günz-Mindel interglacial and during the Mindel glaciation, some more-developed instruments with bifacial flaking appeared and were attributed to *Archanthropus*.

The Middle Paleolithic was characterized by the production of flake instruments; this industry, partly derived from, and chronologically overlapping, that typical of the Lower Paleolithic appeared in the Riss-Würm interglacial and remained during the major part of the Würm glaciation.

Attributed to the palaeanthropines, the flake industry was diffused throughout the northern hemisphere and appears relatively uniform in typology.

The Upper Paleolithic, beginning 35,000 years ago was characterized by the prevailing blade industry, whose authors were members of the *Neanthropus* family to whom are also attributed a parallel tool industry using bones, horn, and ivory, the use of colorants, and in a temperate period of the Würm glaciation (15,000 years ago) the execution of rock paintings.

PALYNOLOGY The study of pollen grains; the presence of fossil pollens made it possible to recognize the vegetable species and the climatic conditions of a deposit.

PEBBLE CULTURE Lithic industry of the Lower Paleolithic period. It includes primitive implements roughly flaked on a single face (choppers) and on two faces (chopping tools). Attributed to *Australanthropus*.

PEKING MAN *Archanthropus* found in the deposit of Choukoutien. These remains consist of 14 cranial caps, 11 jaws, of both sexes and in various states of preservation, 147 teeth and fragments of postcranial bones. The best known cranium has a flat face (platycephalic), prominent brow ridges, and a considerable retro-orbital narrowing; the cranial capacity varies from 915 to 1225 cubic centimeters. There is a strong occipital hollow where the muscle joins the neck. The dental arch is parabolic without diastemata; the upper canines are large and often protrude from the line of occlusion of the denture.

PERFORATOR An instrument made from a blade or from a flake; it has a sharp point at one or at both ends, obtained by hammering or pressure.

small flint objects small hatchet sickle

PITHECANTHROPUS A generic name referring to *Homo erectus*.

POINT Stone implement in subtriangular form; shaped by skillful indirect hammering on the edge of the nucleus. The

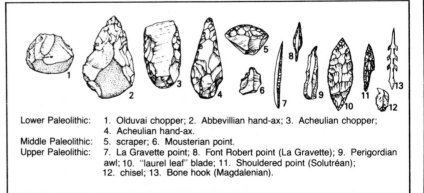

Lower Paleolithic: 1. Olduvai chopper; 2. Abbevillian hand-ax; 3. Acheulian chopper; 4. Acheulian hand-ax.
Middle Paleolithic: 5. scraper; 6. Mousterian point.
Upper Paleolithic: 7. La Gravette point; 8. Font Robert point (La Gravette); 9. Perigordian awl; 10. "laurel leaf" blade; 11. Shouldered point (Solutréan); 12. chisel; 13. Bone hook (Magdalenian).

presence of a shaft facilitates the fixing of a handle.

PONGIDS A family of the order Primates. It includes the genuses *Pan* (chimpanzee), *Gorilla* (gorilla), and *Pongo* (orangutan). The pongids are the living primates which present the greatest affinity with the human species.

POSTCRANIAL Referring to the skeleton with the exclusion of the cranium.

PRESAPIENS See *Palaeanthropus.*

PRIMATES Order of mammals, noted in the fossil state from the beginning of the Tertiary period, to which belong apes, prehominids, and hominids.

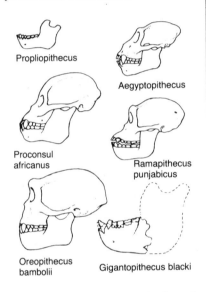

Propliopithecus

Aegyptopithecus

Proconsul africanus

Ramapithecus punjabicus

Oreopithecus bambolii

Gigantopithecus blacki

PROGNATHISM Anterior projection of the jaw resulting from the development of the dental arch; it is somewhat pronounced in the chimpanzee and in the more archaic forms of hominids and practically absent in present-day man.

QUATERNARY Last of the geological eras. It is characterized by great climatic instability. Relatively brief with respect to previous ages (2 million years), it has seen a succession of four glaciations during which the variations in climate and in the level of the seas have caused important modifications in the flora and fauna. The Quaternary era has been subdivided into Pleistocene (epoch of the four glaciations) and Olocene (postglacial period now in progress).

RACE The species *Homo sapiens* is a taxonomic unit subdivided in interfecundate species morphologically different from each other and distributed in various geographic regions. The individual races are generally defined according to such differences in appearance as stature, skin color, type of hair, etc.

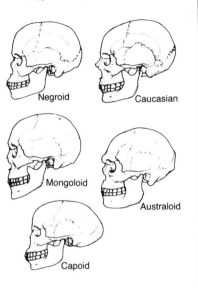

Negroid

Caucasian

Mongoloid

Australoid

Capoid

RELATIVE CHRONOLOGY Determines the stratification and the antiquity of the terrain, without indicating the age in number of years.

SAGITTAL CREST Bony protuberance situated at the center of the cranium roof. It is present in some primates. It encloses the two temporal muscles.

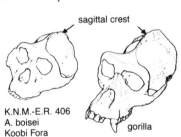

sagittal crest

K.N.M.-E.R. 406
A. boisei
Koobi Fora

gorilla

STRATIGRAPHY Branch of geology concerned with the sequence of the deposition of sediments. Analysis of the stratigraphy permits the recognition of the succession of geological phenomena and, through the remains, information regarding the fauna and flora and any eventual human occupation.

THROWING STICK A hunting weapon in use in recent times among the Eskimos and Australian aborigines. It consists of a stick with one end curved into the shape of a hook; held by the other end it represents an extension of the arm thereby giving greater force to the launching of the javelin. Some prehistoric objects cut from reindeer horn and often richly carved have been thought to be throwing sticks.

VILLAFRANCHIAN PERIOD Period of transition between the Tertiary and Quaternary extending from 4 to 1 million years ago. Named after the deposits at Villafranca d'Asti, Italy. The fauna includes the archaic form of trunked animal (Mastodon) and horse (Equus stenonis).

WALL ART The complex of wall paintings on rock walls.

The Olduvai Gorge, Tanzania
The four strata of the deposit and the
principal finds of fossil hominids.

LOCALITY	SIGN	NAME	AGE
LLK 2	OH 9	H. erectus	0.5
FLK 2 Maiko Gully	OH 16	H. erectus (?)	1.2
MNK 2	OH 13	H. habilis	1
FLK Main	OH 5	A. boisei	1.75
FLK NN 1	OH 7	H. habilis	1.75
FLK NN 1	OH 8	H. habilis	1.75
DK 1	OH 24	H. habilis	1.85
DK 1	STONECIRCLE (living floor)		1.85

Stratum 4 / Stratum 3 / Stratum 2 / Stratum 1

in millions of years

BASALT

Bibliography

AA.VV. *Viaggio nel tempo. Evoluzione dell'uomo e preistoria.* Milano, Le Scienze, 1977.

AGUIRRE E. *L'uomo e la sua evoluzione.* Novara, Ist. Geog. De Agostini, 1977.

ATTENBOROUGH D. *La vita sulla terra.* Milano, Rizzoli, 1979.

BORDES F. *L'antica età della pietra.* Milano, Il Saggiatore, 1968.

BRAY W. e TRUMP D. *Dizionario di Archeologia.* Milano, Mondadori, 1973.

BREZILLON M. *Dizionario della Preistoria.* Torino, S.E.I., 1973.

BROOM R. *Alla ricerca dell'anello mancante.* Milano, Feltrinelli, 1955.

CHIARELLI B. *L'origine dell'uomo.* Roma-Bari, Laterza, 1978.

CLARCK G. *La preistoria del mondo.* Milano, Garzanti, 1967.

COLLINS D. *L'avventura della preistoria.* Roma, Newton Compton, 1980.

COON C.S. *Storia dell'uomo.* Milano, Garzanti, 1956.

DAY M.H. *Guide to Fossil Man.* Londra, Cassel, 1965.

DART R. *The osteodontokeratic culture af Autralopithecus prometheus.* Pretoria, Transvaal Museum, Mem. n. 10, Genn. 1957.

DELCOR M. *Réflection sur l'inscription phénicienne de Nora en Sardaigne.*

DOBZHANSKY T. *L'evoluzione della specie umana.* Torino, Einaudi, 1965.

DU CLEUZIOU E. *La creazione dell'uomo.* Milano, Sonzogno.

FURON R. *Manuale di preistoria.* Torino, Einaudi, 1961.

GIESELER W. *Abstammungskunde des menschen.* Oehringen, Hoenloesche Buchandlung, F. Rau, 1936.

GLYNN I. *La spartizione del cibo negli ominidi protoumani,* in *Le Scienze,* n. 118 (Giugno 1978).

GRASSÈ P.P. *Traité de Zoologie.* Tomo XVI e XVII. Paris, Masson e C., 1968.

GRAZIOSI P. *L'arte preistorica in Italia.* Firenze, Sansoni, 1973.

HARTMANN R. *Le scimmie antropomorfe e la loro organizzazione in confronto con quella dell'uomo.* Milano, 1884.

KEITH A. *New discoveries relating to antiquity of Man.* Londra, William & Norgate L.T.D., 1931.

KOENIGSWALD, VON G.H.R. *Incontro con l'uomo preistorico.* Milano, Il Saggiatore, 1967.

KUHN H. *L'uomo nell'età glaciale.* Milano, Martello, 1954.

KUHN H. *Ritrovamenti ed arte dell'epoca glaciale.* Roma, ed. Mediterranee, 1966.

KUHN H. *Eiszeitmalerei.* Monaco, R. Piper & Co Verlag, 1956.

KURTEN B. *Non dalle scimmie.* Torino, Einaudi, 1972.

JELINEK J. *La grande enciclopedia illustrata dell'uomo preistorico.* Praga, Artia, 1975.

JOHANSON D. e EDEY M. *Lucy, le origini dell'umanità.* Milano, Mondadori, 1981.

van LAWICK-GOODALL J. *L'ombra dell'uomo.* Milano, Rizzoli, 1974.

LEAKEY L.S.B., LEAKEY M.D. *Recent discoveries of fossil hominid in Tankanyka; at Olduvai Gorge and near Lake Natron,* in *Nature,* vol. 202, 4-4, 1964.

LEAKEY L.S.B., TOBIAS P.V., NAPIER J.R. *A new species of the genus Homo from Olduvai Gorge,* in *Nature,* vol. 202, 4-4, 1964.

LEAKEY L.S.B. *Lower dentition of Kenyapithecus africanus,* in *Nature,* vol. 217, 2-3, 1968.

LEAKEY L.S.B. e GOODALL V.M. *La scoperta delle origini dell'uomo.* Milano, Feltrinelli, 1973.

LEAKEY R.E. e LEWIN R. *Origini. Nascita e possibile futuro dell'uomo.* Roma-Bari, Laterza, 1979.

LE GROS CLARK W.E. *The antecedents of Man.* Edinburgh, Edinburgh University Press, 1959.

LE GROS CLARK W.E. *Uomini-Scimmia.* Milano, Feltrinelli, 1973.

LE GROS CLARK W.E. *Hystory of the Primates.* Londra, Trustees of the British Museum, 1970.

LEHMAN J.P. *Le prove paleontologiche dell'evoluzione.* Roma, Newton Compton, 1977.

LEROI-GOURHAN A. *Gli uomini della preistoria.* Milano, Feltrinelli, 1961.

MONTAGU M.F. ASHLEY *An introduction to Physical anthropology.* U.S.A., C. Thomas, 1960.

NESTURK M. *L'origine dell'uomo.* Milano, TETI, 1972.

PADOA E. *Storia della vita sulla terra.* Milano, Feltrinelli, 1959.

PIVETEAU J. *Traité de Paleontologie - Tomo VII.* Parigi, Masson e C., 1957.

PFEIFFER J.E. *La nascita dell'uomo.* Milano, Mondadori, 1971.

RUGE G. *Die Gesichtsmuskulatur der primaten,* Leipzig, 1887.

SCHULTZ A.H. *I Primati.* Milano, Garzanti, 1974.

SIMONS E.L. *New fossil ape from Egypt and the initial differentiation of hominoidea.* in *Nature,* vol 205, 1-9, 1965.

SIMONS E.L. *Ramapithecus,* in *Le Scienze,* n. 109 (sett. 1977).

SPERINO G. *Anatomia del Cimpanzé.* Torino, Unione Tipografico-Editrice, 1897-98.

TOBIAS P.V. *Olduvai Gorge: the cranium of the Australopithecus (Zinjanthropus) Boisei.* Cambridge, Univ. Press., 1-252, 1967.

TRINKAUS E., HOWELLS W.W. *Gli uomini di Neanderthal,* in *Le scienze,* n. 138 (febb. 1980).

UCKO P.J. *Arte Paleolitica.* Milano, Il Saggiatore, 1967.

WAECHTER J. *L'uomo nella preistoria.* Roma, Newton Compton, 1979.

WALKER A., LEAKEY R.E. *Gli Ominidi del Turkana orientale,* in *Le Scienze,* n. 122 (ott. 1978).

WEINER J.S. *L'origine dell'uomo.* Milano, Garzanti, 1974.

WEINERT H. *L'homme preistorique.* Parigi, Payot, 1939.

WOLF J. e BURIAN Z. *L'uomo della preistoria.* Milano, Fabbri, 1978.

YOUNG J. *Biologia, Evoluzione, Cultura.* Torino, Boringhieri, 1970.

CATALOGO DELLA MOSTRA: *Origines de l'homme.* Musée de l'Homme, Parigi, 1976.

CATALOGO DELLA MOSTRA: *Origini dell'uomo.* Università degli studi di Roma. Museo delle origini. Roma, Palombi, 1981.

CATALOGO DELLA MOSTRA: *5 miliardi di anni. Ipotesi per un museo della Scienza.* Palazzo delle Esposizioni, Roma. Multigrafica 1981.

Sources

CONTINENTAL DRIFT Re-elaboration after B. Chiarelli (quoted work)

THE WEAPONS OF OTHER ANIMALS Re-elaboration after specimens exhibited at the Civic Museum of Zoology, Rome

OLDUVAI TOOL INDUSTRY Chopper, drawing after M. Brézillon (quoted work)

HOMOERECTUS TOOL INDUSTRY drawing after F. Bordes (quoted work); R. E. Leakey and R. Lewin (quoted work); and J. Jelínek (quoted work)

HEIDELBERG JAW Institute of Anthropology, Università degli Studi, Florence (cast)

FOOTPRINT OF TERRA AMATA drawing after J. Waechter (quoted work)

THE FOURTH GLACIATION drawing after B. Chiarelli (quoted work)

THE CIRCEO BURIAL Institute of Anthropology, Università degli Studi, Florence (cast)

HUT AND STATUETTES FROM DOLNI VĚSTOVICE statuettes below drawn after J. Jelínek (quoted work)

VENUS OF DOLNI VĚSTOVICE original drawing after a frontal photograph by J. Jelínek (quoted work)

RETOUCHING BY PRESSURE Solutréan point after F. Bordes (quoted work)

CONCHOIDIAL drawn after the original

SKULLS left: Civic Museum of Zoology, Rome; right: Institute of Anthropology, Università degli Studi, Florence

SAGITTAL CREST KNM 406 Institute of Anthropology, University of Rome (cast)

DENTAL ARCH from left, above: Civic Museum of Zoology, Rome; Le scienze, *Viaggio nel tempo,* 1977; K. Gregory and M. Hellmann, *Animals of the Transvaal Museum,* vol. 19 part 4; P. V. Tobias (quoted work); G. H. R. von Koenigswal (quoted work); Institute of Anthropology, University of Florence; Museum of Origins, University of Rome (cast); Institute of Anthropology, University of Rome

M. Brézillon (quoted work)

SKULLS Display-case Institute of Anthropology, Università degli Studi, Florence: Taung, Heidelberg, Montmaurin, Steinheim, Saccopastore I, Saccopastore II, Gibraltar, La-Chapelle-aux-Saints, Monte Circeo I, Le Moustier, Cro-Magnon
Institute of Anthropology, Università degli Studi, Rome: Sterkfontein V, KNM-ER 406 KNM-ER 1470 (drawings after casts).
Museum of Origins, University of Rome: KNM-ER 3883 Peking Arago II Arago XXI (drawings after casts). D. Johanson and M. Edey *Lucy: The Beginnings of Humankind* New York, Simon & Schuster 1981: Hadar
J. Piveteau, *Traité de Paléonthologie* (vol. VII) Paris, Masson & C., 1957: Swartkrans, Swanscombe, La Ferrassie I, La Quina (inf.), Spy I, Takun, Es Skuhl V, Combe-Capelle, Předmostí, Afalou-bou-Rummel, Grimaldi
Ashley M. F. Montagu, *An Introduction to Physical Anthropology.* U.S.A., Thomas, 1960: Sterkfontein, Makapansgat, Kromdraai, Solo (Java), Saldanha W.
Gieseler *Abstammungskunde des Menschen.* Oheringen, Hoenloesche Buchhandlung F. Rau, 1936: Java, Peking, Oberkassel
M. H. Day, *Guide to Fossil Man.* London, Cassel, 1977 (3rd edition): Swartkrans SK 48, KNM-ER 732, KNM-ER 1813, OH9 Olduvai, Petralona, Krapina, Amud I, Kafzeh, Ighoud
B. Chiarelli, *L'origine dell'uomo.* Roma-Bari, Laterza 1978: P. IV Java
J. Jelínek, *La grande enciclopedia illustrata dell'uomo preistorico.* Prague, Artia, 1975 (Italian edition Librerie Accademia S.p.A.): Teshik-Tash, Shanidar
M. Nesturk, *L'origine dell'uomo.* Milan, N. Teti, 1972; Kostenki XIV
P. V. Tobias, *Olduvai Gorge.* Cambridge, University Press, 1967: OH 5 Olduvai

HOMINOIDEA Civic Museum of Zoology, Rome (drawings of the skulls)

PALEOLOTHICUM Redesigned after M. Brézillon (quoted work) (1–13); F. Bordes (quoted work) (8)

PRIMATES Jelínek (quoted work) and Institute of Anthropology, University of Rome (last drawing below, right)

RACE Institute of Anthropology, University of Florence (drawings of the skulls)

FLAKING above, redesigned after M. Brézillon (quoted work); below, redesigned after A. Leroi-Gourhan (quoted work)

STRATIGRAPHY Elaboration after J. Waechter (quoted work) and M. N. Day (quoted work)